Ancient Techniques of Rune Magic

This book is about the magical alphabet of the North European peoples—its background, history, use in ritual and divination, and its meaning. The runes are fully integrated into modern Western occult practice. A fascinating ritual method is presented which clearly shows how a rune ritual may be patterned.

Drawing upon historical records, poetic fragments, and the informed study of scholars, *Rune Magic* resurrects the ancient techniques of rune magic which until now have generally been assumed lost in time. It integrates these methods with modern occultism so that anyone can fit the runes into a personal magical system. It gives for the first time all known and conjectured meanings of all 33 extant runes.

A complete mythic background is presented that places the runes in the context in which they evolved and were used. In addition, a concise mnemonic exposition of the magical method is provided that will prove invaluable to anyone trying to understand how magic is worked. The ancient method of divination by rune wands is clearly explained, along with two easier and more modern methods using cards and dice.

A technique of mirror skrying—which has rarely been revealed with any degree of clarity—is offered whereby the runes may be explored astrally, and 24 rune worlds are outlined.

All the known information on the ancient meaning and use of the runes is condensed in a readable and easily accessible format, allowing you to arrive at your own personal understanding of rune magic.

About Donald Tyson

Donald Tyson was born around midnight, January 12, 1954, in the province of Nova Scotia in eastern Canada, where he presently resides. His writings range from radio and television drama to juvenile novels, but his true vocation is magic. When he was a child he often regretted that the stories about vampires, werewolves, and ghosts were not true. When he grew older and more foolish, he realized they were true and that materialism was a lie. Since then, he has set about pulling the blinders of science off as many heads as possible. He is a true Capricorn by birth and nature. His *I Ching* hexagram is Sung.

To Write to the Author

If you wish to contact the author or would like more information about this book, please write to the author in care of Llewellyn Worldwide, and we will forward your request. Both the author and publisher appreciate hearing from you and learning of your enjoyment of this book and how it has helped you. Llewellyn Worldwide cannot guarantee that every letter written to the author can be answered, but all will be forwarded. Please write to:

Donald Tyson
c/o Llewellyn Worldwide
P.O. Box 64383-826, St. Paul, MN 55164-0383, U.S.A.

Please enclose a self-addressed, stamped envelope for reply, or $1.00 to cover costs.
If outside the U.S.A., enclose international postal reply coupon.

Free Catalog from Llewellyn

For more than 90 years Llewellyn has brought its readers knowledge in the fields of metaphysics and human potential. Learn about the newest books in spiritual guidance, natural healing, astrology, occult philosophy and more. Enjoy book reviews, new age articles, a calendar of events, plus current advertised products and services. To get your free copy of *Llewellyn's New Worlds*, send your name and address to:

Llewellyn's New Worlds of Mind and Spirit
P.O. Box 64383-826, St. Paul, MN 55164-0383, U.S.A.

About Llewellyn's Practical Magick Series

To some people, the idea that "Magick" is *practical* comes as a suprise.

It shouldn't. The entire basis for Magick is to exercise influence over one's environment. While Magick is also, and properly so, concerned with spiritual growth and psychological transformation—even the spiritual life must rest firmly on material foundations.

The material world and the psychic are intertwined, and it is this very fact that establishes the Magickal Link: that the psychic can as easily influence the material as vice versa.

Magick can, and should, be used in one's daily life for better living! Each of us has been given Mind and Body, and surely we are under Spiritual obligation to make full usage of these wonderful gifts. Mind and Body work together, and Magick is simply the extension of this interaction into dimensions beyond the limits normally conceived. That's why we commonly talk of the "supernormal" in connection with domain of Magick.

The Body is alive, and all Life is an expression of the Divine. There is God-power in the Body and in the Earth, just as there is in Mind and Spirit. With Love and Will, we use Mind to link these aspects of Divinity together to bring about change.

With Magick we increase the flow of Divinity in our lives and in the world around us. We add to the beauty of it all—for to work Magick we must work in harmony with the Laws of Nature and of the Psyche. *Magick is the flowering of the Human Potential.*

Practical Magick is concerned with the Craft of Living well and in harmony with Nature, and with the Magick of the Earth, in the things of the Earth, in the seasons and cycles and in the things we make with hand and Mind.

Other Books by Donald Tyson

The New Magus, 1988
The Truth About Ritual Magic, 1989
The Truth About Runse, 1989
How to Make and Use a Magic Mirror, 1990
Ritual Magic, 1992
The Messenger, 1993

Cards and Kits

Rune Magic Deck, 1988
Power of the Runes, 1989

Editor and Annotator

Three Books of Occult Philosophy Written by Henry Cornelius Agrippa of Nettesheim, 1993

Llewellyn's Practical Magick Series

RUNE MAGIC

Donald Tyson

1995
Llewellyn Publications
St. Paul, Minnesota 55164-0383, U.S.A.

Cover painting: Martin Cannon

FIRST EDITION
Seventh Printing, 1995

Library of Congress Cataloging-in-Publication Data
    Tyson, Donald, 1954-
        Rune magic.
    (Llewellyn's practical magick series)
    1. Magic. 2 Runes—Miscellanea. 3. Fortune-telling runes.
    I. Title   II. Series
    BF1623.R89T97   1988   133.4'3   87-45741
    ISBN 0-87542-826-6

Llewellyn Publications
A Division of Llewellyn Worldwide, Ltd.
P.O. 64383, St. Paul, MN 55164-0383

Contents

Chapter 1

GODS AND GODDESSES

OF THE RUNES

The Teutons—a general name for the tribes of peoples who lived in the forests of northern Europe, including the Germans, Goths and Anglo-Saxons—were a stern, unyielding race whose chief delight lay in making war. Before the coming of Christianity they shared a common language and culture. They viewed the world and the gods in familiar terms. The world was a harsh proving ground, and the gods were a kind of superior race of men worthy of admiration because they knew best how to gain their will against the cruelty of elemental forces.

In the beginning, Teutonic legends say, was a void. No ocean rolled through its vast emptiness. No tree raised its boughs or deepened its roots. To the north beyond the abyss formed a region of cloud and shadow called Niflheim. To the south formed a land of fire, Muspellsheim. Twelve rivers of pure glacial water flowed out of Niflheim and met corresponding rivers from Muspellsheim—but these were filled with bitter poison and soon solidified. When the icy waters of the north touched their rigid serpentine bodies, the abyss was filled with prickly hoarfrost.

1

Warm air blowing up from the south began to melt the frost, and from the mingled waters arose Ymir, a frost giant, the first of all living beings, described in a translation of the *Prose Edda:*

> . . . and when the breath of heat met the frost, so that it melted and dripped, life was quickened from the yeast-drops by the power of that which sent the heat, and became a man's form.

The ice also gave birth to a great cow named Audumla, and Ymir would slack his thirst on the four streams of milk that flowed from this creature. Each of these primal beings produced children asexually—Ymir from his sweat and Audumla by licking the ice with her tongue. The marriage of Bestla, daughter of Ymir, with Bor, grandson of Audumla, produced the three gods Odin, Vili and Va, who at once turned on the race of giants and slaughtered all but two who escaped to perpetuate the race.

The three gods raised the inert body of Ymir out of the waters of chaos that had flowed from the melting ice and created the earth, which they called Midgard, the Middle Abode. Of Ymir's bones the mountains were made, and his blood filled up the ocean. His flesh became the land and his hairs the trees. With his skull the gods formed the vault of heaven, which they filled with bright sparks from the fires of Muspellsheim. The sparks are the stars and planets.

From the soil sprang the great ash tree Yggdrasill whose mighty branches separate the heavens from the earth and whose trunk is the axis of the universe. Indeed in some legends Yggdrasill itself is the world. No man can tell its greatness. Its roots reach deeper than the roots of mountains and its evergreen leaves catch the whirling stars as they pass.

Its roots are three. The first reaches to Niflheim, land of shadows which is the underworld, and touches the fountain Hvergelmir where spring the twelve northern rivers. The second enters the land of the frost giants and drinks of the fountain of Mimir, source of all wisdom. The third extends into the heavens where flows the fountain of Urd, wisest of the Norns—strange creatures who judge the fate of all beings.

Many forces attack the sacred ash. Four stags nibble off its new buds before they turn green. The steed of Odin, Sleipnir, browses on its foliage. The goat Heidrun is nourished by its leaves. Worst of all the serpent Nidhogg, a vast monster, ceaselessly gnaws away at its root. Only the loving care of the Norns preserve it. Each day they draw water from the fountain of Urd and sprinkle it on Yggdrasill to keep it flourishing.

From the grubs in the rotting flesh of Ymir, the gods made the race of dwarfs who are destined to dwell forever in the depths of the earth. Since they are all made, they cannot procreate. When a dwarf dies, a new dwarf is molded from the stones and soil by two dwarf-princes created for this purpose.

Man and woman were made from the trunks of two lifeless trees. Odin blew life into them. The god Hoenir gave them a soul and the power of reason. Lodur gave them warmth and beauty. The man was called Ask (Ash) and the woman Embla (Vine), and from them the human race is descended.

As the mythology of the Teutonic peoples developed, it gradually took on a more definite shape. The world was seen as a flat disk surrounded by a single ocean. In the ocean lived the serpent of Midgard whose coils circled the earth. Above Midgard was Asgard, the abode of the Aesir, or gods, which was joined to the realm of men by Bifrost, the Rainbow Bridge. Below Midgard lay the region of the dead, Niflheim (mist-world). It is the same place that in earlier mythology was said to lie in the north, but adapted to serve the more complex vision of the evolving universe.

In dealing with mythology it is difficult to avoid confusion because what is true at one epoch in the changing consciousness of a race may not remain so later in its development. This will be seen clearly in the descriptions of the gods, who change dramatically over the course of their existence.

Odin, or Woden as the Germans called him, began life as a minor deity of the night storms who rode furiously across the sky with a troop of mysterious horsemen, the ghosts of dead warriors. *Wode* means fury, the release of the blind forces of nature. On stormy nights the thunder of his mount's hooves was said to be heard ringing above the clouds.

Later as the god began to form in the minds of his people, he was seen as the master of brute forces, not as a brute force himself. He ruled these wild powers through his skill in magic and peered deep into all secret things. He was not a warrior, but directed the outcome of battles for his own ends, using his *herfjoturr*, or army fetter—a spell causing a paralyzing fear in the ranks of his enemies. For this reason warriors worshipped him. He was also god of medicine and healed the sick and wounded.

He would walk the length of the earth in the guise of a road-stained traveler with a broad brimmed hat, or hood, pulled low to hide his empty eye socket. He had sacrificed his eye gaining wisdom from the fountain of Mimir and was known as the One-eyed God. A long cloak swirled from his shoulders. Two wolves ran at his sides to act as his guardians and emissaries. Two crows flew before him and returned to whisper secrets in his ears. One was named Thought and the other Memory. The Anglo-Saxons knew the god in this form as Grim, the Hooded One.

Later still in his evolution Odin was seen as a wise law-maker who directed the affairs of gods and men. All who heard him were overcome by his eloquence. He was skilled in poetry and handsome of face. He wore a gleaming breastplate and a golden helmet, and carried the dwarf-forged spear Gungnir which always found its mark. The palace of the god was called Valhalla. Here Odin presided over the heroes who had died in earthly battles.

However, even at his most regal and judicial, Odin never entirely loses his roots. He can be capricious in the dispensation of his favors and abruptly desert a warrior he has previously protected. He is given to unreasoning rage and is prey to the sins of the flesh—no goddess, giantess or mortal woman is safe from his amorous advances.

It was Odin who discovered the runes by performing a ritual of self-sacrifice. First he gashed his body with the point of his spear, then bound himself to Yggdrasill. For nine days he refused all food and drink. Finally, he was able to peer down into the very depths of being, where he saw the runic characters.

Odin by Fogelberg. Ink and wash sketch.
The arch of his throne forms the starry heavens of his sovereignty. Runes are
carved on the sheath of his sword. Gungnir is in his right hand. His familiar
crows sit on either side to whisper news from far off lands.

With a cry he reached down and clasped them. The strain was so great that the god fainted, but he held onto the runes and they are his legacy to the present.

The Romans associated Odin with Mercury because of his magical powers and great learning. He was assigned the weekday *Mercurii dies*, which in the north became Wednesday. However, Odin is a complex being. It would be legitimate to associate him with Mars since he is god of *wode* and lord of battle. Equally, he might be linked with Jupiter since both Jupiter and Odin are lawgivers and patriarchs. This last role, father of heaven, is the one that Odin is most closely linked with in the final stage of his worship.

In many parts of the pagan world, Thor was a more significant deity than Odin. It may have been that the warlike and independent Teutons appreciated his supreme battle prowess and were willing to overlook his shortcomings. Perhaps the early Thor had more noble qualities than the blustering, clownish oaf that has come down to the present through the Norse tales and sagas.

The early Thor, named Donar, was a fearsome storm god. When the thunder rolled it was said to be the great wheels of Donar's chariot. When lightning struck it was a fiery hammer cast by the god onto the earth. In his elemental rawness Donar bears much similarity with the early Woden. Nothing is known of the appearance of Donar, since the German poetry that might have described him was never written down.

In the Scandinavian lands, Donar becomes Thor and takes on a brutish appearance. He is coarse of feature and manner with wild dark hair, a ruddy complexion and flashing eyes filled with battle lust. His weapon is the hammer Mjolnir, the Destroyer, which was perhaps first conceived as a meteorite fallen from the heavens, but later was said to be the work of dwarfs. In the early legends it was made of stone; later it became iron. His weapon suggests the character of the god: a spear or sword pierces, an axe cuts, but a hammer merely bashes.

Thor was associated with Jupiter because of his ability to hurl thunderbolts, and *Jovis dies* became Thursday. Actually, the god most similar to Thor in the Roman days of the week is Mars. Both are gods of battle and find it impossible to restrain their fury when the fighting starts. Both delight in slaying and combat.

In the *Iliad*, Zeus says to Aries (the Greek Mars): "Of all the gods who live on Olympus thou art the most odious to me; for thou enjoyest nothing but strife, war and battle." This might easily have been spoken by Odin to Thor.

On occasion, Odin showed his contempt for Thor's rough manners and dull wits. Once on a whim Odin impersonated a ferryman and refused to allow Thor to cross an inlet of the sea. "Peasant," said Odin, "You are only a penniless vagabond, a barefooted beggar, a brigand and a horse-thief. My ferry is not for the likes of you."

The third in the great trinity of masculine warrior deities is Tiw, or Tyr. Since his cult was eclipsed early on by those of Odin and Thor, little is known about his beginnings or appearance. Originally he was a god of judgment and legal matters. His spear served as an emblem of judicial authority and he presided over the *thing*, the tribal assembly where laws were applied. He was said to be courageous and resourceful. It was Tiw who often decided the outcome of mortal battles, and for this reason warriors invoked his name.

One story has survived that gives insight into his character. The gods decided to chain up the giant wolf Fenrir and had dwarfs forge a chain that no creature could break. Then they enticed Fenrir to put on the chain as a test of his strength. Suspecting a trap, the wolf agreed on condition that one of the gods place his hand in the wolf's jaws. Since the gods knew Fenrir would be enraged when he discovered he had been deceived, none would volunteer until Tiw stepped forward and calmly put his right hand in the wolf's mouth. As soon as Fenrir discovered he could not break the chain and saw the gods mocking him, he bit off Tiw's hand at the wrist, and thereafter the god was called the One-handed.

The significant elements of the story are Tiw's courage, his sense of responsibility, and his acceptance of the terms set by the wolf. He was instrumental in the fulfillment of the legal contract

Freyja Seeking her Husband by Blommer. Oil painting on canvas.
Freyja is wed to a god named Od, who goes away on long journeys. She weeps for him tears of red gold, and seeks after him in a chariot drawn by two cats, using many names as concealments. She is called Mardoll, Horn, Gefn (Giver) and Syr (Sow). It is said that she is most readily invoked, enjoys poetry, and will give help when asked in love affairs. Notice the rune staff in her hand, on which the artist has signed his name.

between Fenrir and the gods, a function of the highest importance in the ongoing stability of the universe.

Tiw was associated with the planetary god Mars. *Martis dies*
became Tuesday. This relationship is only acceptable when Tiw
is perceived as a minor god of war. Before his degeneration, Tiw
was much nearer in character to the god of wisdom, Mercury.
Both possess nobility and prudence. Both are instruments of a
higher order.

Frey was a member of the race of gods known as Vanir, who
were at one time rivals of the Aesir—to which Odin, Thor and
Tiw belonged—then later became their allies. Originally, he
must have been a fertility god, but in the Norse poetry he is
humanized and trivialized. He owns a magic sword that cuts the
air of its own accord and a ship that voyages straight to its des-
tination the moment its sail is hoisted. Little is known about his
appearance, but by all accounts he is noble and brave.

Frey means Lord. His feminine counterpart is named Freyja—
Lady. Essentially, they are the male and female aspects of the
generative power of the earth, perhaps carry-overs from the
earlier god pair Nerthus-Njord.

Goddesses are not so numerous as gods in Teutonic mythology. The most often mentioned is the wife of Odin, Frija, which
means Well-beloved. She shares some of her husband's wisdom
but is not always in agreement with him. Frija is not above
scheming to get her own way. If she takes a liking to a warrior
Odin has fated to fall in battle, the outcome is never certain.

In her earliest form, Frija was a goddess of fertility and
marriage. Her name was invoked to bring children. Like most
fertility goddesses she is promiscuous. The Romans identified
her with Venus, and *Veneris dies* became Friday.

Frija is confused in the myths with Freyja because of the
similarity of their names. Whereas Frija is an Aesir, Freyja is a
Vanir and the leader of the Valkyries. However, the characters of
Frija and Freyja have the same root in the feminization of an
earth deity. They act from similar motives and are bound closely
to Frey in all matters apart from their sex. A story told about
Freyja might easily suit Frija as well.

One day Freyja was visiting the workshop of the dwarfs when she saw on a table a necklace of surpassing beauty and cunning craft. The goddess, who loved adornment above all things, offered anything to possess the necklace. The dwarfs agreed to give her the necklace only on the condition that she pass one night with each of them. Immediately Freyja consented. When Odin heard about the bargain he was so shocked that he had Loki steal the necklace from around Freyja's neck while she slept, and gave it back only after making her agree to provoke a war between two mortal kings.

A more dignified goddess is Nerthus, a personification of the Mother Earth, also called Hertha or Eartha. When she was ritually drawn around her sacred island in a veiled chariot, all swords remained in their scabbards. Quarreling was punished by death. After the invisible goddess had been restored to her sanctuary by her priests, the chariot was cleansed of impurities in the sea and all who took part in the washing were drowned. The festival of Nerthus was celebrated in the spring.

The goddess Hel has a much different personality. She rules Niflheim, the mist world of the dead where strange monsters dwell. She is said to be the daughter of Loki, raised in the land of giants. She gives asylum to the serpent Nidhogg who gnaws the root of Yggdrasill. Her appearance is terrifying. Her head hangs forward on her shoulders. Half her face is human but the other half is obscured by black shadow. In her palace she presides over great feasts of the dead.

Loki is an important Teutonic deity but is difficult to classify. Originally he seems to have been a fire demon. In Norway when a fire crackles, they say Loki is thrashing his children. His father was the striker of sparks and his mother a wooded isle. Over time Loki grew in stature but he always remained indefinable. On some occasions he helped the gods. Other occasions saw him betray his friends for gain.

He developed from an elementary being into a trickster who delighted to confound the wits of others. Like Odin he was a shape-changer and often took the form of annoying insects such as the gadfly and the flea. A function of his was to shame

Loki and Sigyn by Winge. Oil painting on canvas.
For the slaying of Balder, Loki is bound in a cave beneath a venomous serpent so that its poison drips onto his face. His wife, Sigyn, catches the poison in a bowl, but when the bowl is full and she goes to empty it, the poison strikes his face, and his writhings are the cause of earthquakes.

the gods with remembrance of their past ignoble deeds. Once when the gods held a feast to which he had not been invited, he insinuated himself into the hall and after accepting food and drink proceeded to detail the unfaithfulness of each of their wives.

In the latter stages of his myth Loki became a traitor and a figure of evil very similar to Lucifer. This may be the result of the growth of Christianity, or may simply be his inevitable evolution. He is wickedness for its own sake and commits crimes for the sheer pleasure of it.

Heimdall is a god of light. His name may mean "he who casts bright rays." He presides over the origin of things and stands guard at the entrance to Asgard on Bifrost, the Rainbow Bridge. In assemblies it is Heimdall who speaks first. He is a tall, handsome warrior with teeth of pure gold armed with a sword and mounted on a charger. He requires less sleep than a bird and can see at night. He hears the grass growing on the earth. His trumpet is capable of sounding throughout the entire universe. It lies hidden in the roots of Yggdrasill until the day when it will announce the final conflict between gods and giants.

Heimdall is the enemy of Loki, who mocks the patient god for his kind service. During the final conflict it will be Heimdall who slays Loki, even though he himself will die in the battle. In the abstract, Heimdall signifies the quiet virtues of patience, vigilance and silence without which no kingdom, heavenly or earthly, can long endure.

Another major god of whom little is known is Balder. Like Heimdall he is a god of light. He is said to be the son of Odin and Frija. He is similar to the Greek god Apollo. Because he is so beautiful, a golden radiance shines around him. No other god equals him in wisdom. All who look at him or hear him speak love him at once. Only Loki is immune from Balder's goodness. The trickster hates the radiant one and plots against him.

Once Balder was troubled with dreams in which he received presentiments of his doom. He told the other gods, and Frija, out of love for him, went to all things on heaven and earth and made them swear an oath never to harm Balder. From that instant it seemed that Balder was invulnerable. The other gods made sport by hurling their weapons at him. No projectile or blow caused him the least hurt.

Crafty Loki questioned Frija and discovered that of all things in the world only one had escaped swearing her oath—a small sprig of mistletoe that grew west of Valhalla. At once Loki procured the sprig and tricked a blind warrior named Hod into hurling it at Balder. The mistletoe pierced Balder's heart. The beloved god fell dead.

Shocked but not defeated, the gods sent the son of Odin, Hermod, to the underworld to plead with Hel for Balder's life. After many hardships, he passed the gates of shadow and put his purpose before Hel. Hel was a fearsome but not a malicious goddess. She agreed to release Balder on condition that every living thing mourn for him.

Since all loved Balder, this seemed assured. But Loki, determined to seal his vengeance, transformed himself into a giantess named Thokk and refused to shed tears for the shining god. Thus Balder was condemned to remain in the land of the dead.

The other gods learned of Loki's deceit and put him in chains. Loki broke free and joined the frost giants. Evil omens multiplied. The sun was devoured by a cub of the wolf Fenrir, and the world plunged into darkness and winter. Wars broke out. Brother fought against brother and father against son. Loki stole from Heimdall his sword, and through enchantment clouded the vision of the keen-eyed watcher until the army of giants was almost to the gates of Asgard. Fenrir broke his dwarf-forged chain and joined the giants.

So begins the great battle of *ragna rok* which has been incorrectly called the Twilight of the Gods. *Ragna rok* is Icelandic and means Fatal Destiny. In the 12th century, Norse writers substituted the words *ragna rokkr* which translates as the more colorful Twilight of the Gods. *Ragna rok* is a prophetic vision of the destruction of the universe similar in tone and in many details to the Apocalypse of the New Testament.

Many old scores are settled in the final battle. Thor slays the Midgard serpent, but breathes in so much poison from the monster that he dies. Heimdall slays Loki and dies in the battle. Tiw

Thor's Fight with the Giants by Winge. Oil painting on canvas.
Note the swastika, an ancient Teutonic symbol associated with the flaming
meteor of Thor's hammer, at his belt.

slays Gorm, the guardian hound of the underworld, but again he dies in the fight. Odin is killed almost the moment the battle begins, engulfed in the maw of Fenrir. His son Vidar avenges his father by killing the giant wolf.

The battle is lost. The stars drift from their places and fall into the waves of the sea. Surt, the fire giant, sets the entire world aflame. All living things are scorched and destroyed. The ocean and rivers roil and cover the land. All things seem at an end.

But hope is not entirely extinguished. From the ashes of the old world, a new world will arise. Other gods who have not been involved in the strife between the Aesir and the giants will survive to rule the world. Men and women who have hidden in cracks in the trunk of Yggdrasill, which will not be consumed by the fire, will emerge to repopulate the land. Of the old gods, Balder, the best beloved, will be reborn and preside over the great hall where Odin formerly sat.

In addition to the gods and monsters of greater mythology, the Teutons believed in a variety of lesser supernatural beings. Ghosts were supposed by some to linger around the places of burial, and for this reason honored dead were buried under the threshold of their houses to act as guardian spirits. Ghosts who had a guilty conscience were believed to not be able to rest until they redressed their offenses.

The souls of the living were thought to lead a semi-independent existence and to leave the bodies that housed them during sleep. These soul-beings were called *fylgjur*, which means Followers. They were material and could mold themselves into the forms of men or animals, travel about and even speak. Clearly they were an early expression of the concept of astral travel, differing from the modern notion in their independent awareness. *Fylgjur* were bound to the bodies that housed them by mystical ties. If either were killed, the other also died.

The Norns are the mistresses of fate. Originally there was only one Norn, but under the classical Roman influence they became three. They control the prosperity or misery of all lives and set the time and place of death. When a child is born they come to the cradle either to bless or curse the offspring. Even the gods are under their authority.

Valkyries are warrior goddesses who preside over the battlefield. They give victory to the side they favor, decide which hero should be taken to Valhalla, and even participate in the battle. Their name means roughly "she who chooses warriors destined to die in battle." They wear helmets, grasp spears crowned with flame and ride flying steeds. Occasionally they become the wives or mistresses of mortal men.

Elves are nature spirits with the shape of human beings, but more delicately formed. They are organized into kingdoms and enjoy nighttime frolics. The sun hurts their eyes and they fear men.

Undines, or water spirits, dwell in springs and rivers and are usually of human appearance. Most are female but some are male. They love to sit in the sun by the banks of streams and rivers. When they see a man they fancy they draw him under the water and drown him. Some who hear their haunting songs lose their reason.

The forests are inhabited by wood spirits who are covered with moss and have faces like gnarled tree bark. Sometimes they help men. They know the secrets of herbs and how to cure sickness, but they have been accused of changing into insects to spread disease.

In houses live familiar spirits of the hearth called *kobolds*. They look like old men in pointed hoods. Usually they live in the cellar or barn, and make themselves useful by performing small chores such as chopping wood and drawing water. A small amount of milk is left out for them as payment to forestall their vindictive spite.

It is through this magic world of greater and lesser supernatural forces that the runes function. To use runes rightly, one must appreciate the environment from which they evolved and the needs and desires of the people who made them. The preceding mythological outline is only a brief sketch. Serious students of rune magic will want to acquaint themselves fully with the Teutonic gods and their stories.

Chapter 2

ORIGIN AND DEVELOPMENT OF RUNES

The poets taught that runes were discovered by Odin beneath the roots of Yggdrasill, the sacred ash that holds up the heavens. Speaking in the eddic *Havamal*, Odin himself says:

> I trow that I hung on the windy tree,
> swing there nights all nine,
> gashed with a blade,
> bloodied for Odin,
> myself a sacrifice to myself—
> knotted to that tree,
> no man knows
> whither the roots of it run.
>
> None gave me bread
> none gave me drink,
> down to the depths
> I peered
> to snatch up runes
> with a roaring scream
> and fell in a dizzied swoon.

> Well-being I won
> and wisdom too,
> I grew and joyed in my growth—
> from a word to a word
> I was led to a word,
> from a deed to another deed.

These lines describe a magical ritual of initiation involving the death of the mundane self and rebirth into the higher mysteries. The position of the god on the tree is that of the Hanged Man of the Tarot—suspended head downward, he peers not only into the depths of the earth but into the depths of his own being. The runes are the sacred symbols of his Higher Self. To possess them is a shattering experience akin to looking into the face of God. But once they are his, all things become possible. His bonds fall off and the weary god drops to the earth, the runes seared upon his heart.

Rune means secret. In German it is related to the word for whispering. In Anglo-Saxon England, a secret gathering of chiefs was called a rune. In modern times any obscure markings are referred to as runes. The word connotes the mysterious, the unknown, the supernatural. This is fitting because runes have always been foremost a magical device, and only secondarily a mode of writing.

The historical creation of runes is analogous to the creation of life in Teutonic myth. Two cultural currents, one from the north and one from the south, met and mingled. From their meeting the runes grew as a tree grows. In time that first plant sent out seeds and other trees—other runic alphabets—took root in different lands.

The northern current, father of the runes, was supernatural. Centuries before the birth of Christ, the Germanic tribes had used symbols as aids in working magic. Some of these are preserved in rock carvings, which bear the technical name *hallristningar*. They are simple and powerful expressions of the fundamental forces of nature:

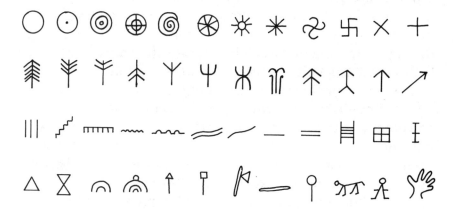

The meanings of many of the symbols can be conjectured. For example, the upward-pointing triangle (△) must have signified some aspect of masculine potency as embodied in nature by the phallus, the mountain, the flame. The tree with five branches (ⵌ) must have been a stylized picture of the splayed hand, which is a universal symbol for warding off evil. Undulating lines close together (⌇) meant water, specifically a river or stream, with the association of the feminine power of nurturing.

Other symbols in the ancient carvings are less readily given a particular meaning. However, merely because the modern world does not understand them, it would be foolish to assume that the shaman who spent hours cutting them into the hard surface of the rock did not know exactly what they signified. Similar signs such as these two forms of sun-wheel (币 and 岙) likely had related, but very distinct, magical uses.

The simplicity of the carvings suggests that they were ancient long before they were recorded. To represent the power of the sun, for example, by a few lines necessitates a whole series of rational jumps. First the primitive man looking at the sun must generalize it as a source of warmth and life. Then he must relate its qualities—brightness, shape, color, motion—to other natural phenomena in order to isolate its unique characteristics.

The stars are bright but have no disk. The moon has a disk but is not warm. Ripe grain is yellow and alive, but is neither radiant nor circular. Having abstracted physical elements that represent the inner meaning of the sun in this way, they must be reduced to those with specific magical uses and represented graphically. This is not a considered process but the work of generations.

Although the rock symbols probably had individual names and functions, there is no evidence they were ever used for writing. The nomadic Germanic tribes would have had little use for a written language. If they ever did develop their own independent form of writing, no example of it has survived.

The southern current, mother of the runes, was the Etruscan—and to a lesser extent the Latin—alphabet. The Etruscans were a hardy, enterprising race of manufacturers and traders who lived in northern Italy. Originally they had come over the Alps from the north. At the time the runes came into being, about 500 B.C., they had mingled with eastern peoples and established a thriving civilization that rivaled Greece. The Greeks of the period looked upon Rome as an Etruscan colony.

It can only be conjectured how elements of the Etruscan alphabet found their way north over the mountains. The best guess is that German mercenaries fighting in northern Italy absorbed some of the Etruscan civilization. To the German shaman the Etruscan letters must have seemed like so many magical symbols. All magicians are eager to add to their stock of knowledge. No doubt the strange symbols were impressive around the home campfire.

Sometime later after the Etruscan letters had mingled with the German rock symbols, the concept of a written language was adopted by the German priest-magicians. They did not want to abandon the old familiar symbols, and besides there were sounds in the German language that were not in Etruscan. A mingling took place in which characters of value from the old and the new were forged into the German *futhark* of 24 letters.

Futhark is a word made up of the first six letters in the German rune aplphabet: ᚠ (F); ᚢ (U); ᚦ (Th); ᚨ (A); ᚱ (R); ᚲ (K).

Some of the correspondences between Etruscan letters and the runes are striking. The Etruscan ⦚ is a reflection of the rune ⟨ (Sigel). Etruscan √ is an inversion of the rune Ր (Lagu). Etruscan ∨ is an inverted version of the rune Λ (Ur). Other factors suggest a link. The earliest Etruscan inscriptions are written in a serpentine pattern back and forth down the writing surface, the way a farmer ploughs a field. Rune inscriptions run right to left, left to right, and invert direction without warning. The characters may face either right or left.

Rock Carvings	Etruscan	Latin	Runes
		F	
		V	
		D	
		A	
		R	
		C	
		X	
		-	
		H	
		N	
		I	
		G	
		-	
		P	
		Z	
		S	
		T	
		B	
		E	
		M	
		L	
		-	
		-	
		O	

Some time after the genesis of the early rune alphabet, perhaps hundreds of years, the rise in the power of Rome made the Latin alphabet more prominent, and elements of Latin were absorbed into the runes. Two characters especially have a strong resemblance to Latin letters, but no strong Etruscan relation: the rune ᛒ (Beorc) is similar to the Latin B; the rune ᚱ (Rad) is like the Latin R.

Runes spread all over Europe, extending as far north as Scandinavia and as far west as Britain. When the Vikings settled Iceland, they carried rune lore with them. Since the hunter societies had little use for writing, runes were mainly employed as pictographs with powerful magical associations. Only the most educated—priests, magicians and perhaps chiefs—can be supposed to have known the secret of writing phonetically with runes. This is one reason why many of the rune relics discovered bear no intelligible words. Their carvers were illiterate. However, they understood the magical meaning of each rune, and how to combine them in certain number series for magical effects.

Lincoln Comb Case. Wood. 11th century.
Part of the litter left in England by the Viking invasions. The runes are Danish and record the name of the comb's maker.

The form of the runes was determined by the lifestyle of the peoples who used them. The Germans had no writing instruments in the early days. Since they moved constantly from one place to another, runes would not be written on stone on a regular basis because stones were too heavy to carry. They could not be written on any costly material except in special circumstances since they would often have to be discarded on the road. Consequently they were shaped to be cut with a knife, axe, arrowhead, or any other sharp edge on the twigs of trees.

All the strokes in the original *futhark* are either vertical or diagonal. Cut across a wood stem they would show up without being obscured by cracks or heavy grain. In cutting them cross-grain, there was no danger of splitting their wooden base. Rounded twigs could be rolled slightly under the blade of a knife to produce in a few minutes many clear, attractive runes. The contrast between the dark outer bark and the lighter wood beneath insured their easy visibility.

Few of these rough rune wands have survived for the simple reason that they were intended to be discarded after use. Perhaps they were even deliberately burned or destroyed as a part of a magical ritual. What has survived are runic inscriptions that soldiers made on their weapons to give them power, jewelry with inscribed charms, amulets for protective or other functions, coins, and epitaphs on stone to mark graves or significant sites.

All these were made well into the Christian era when the Teutonic peoples had settled in fixed localities. The shape of the runes altered to suit changed circumstances. Curved lines appeared. For example, the rune Ͷ (Ur) became ᒥ. Horizontal lines also cropped up. Ing (◇) was sometimes written ☐ . There was no need to avoid curved and horizontal lines when carving runes on stone since stone has no significant grain.

As different peoples with different languages adopted runes, they altered them to suit their needs. The rune alphabet was expanded and contracted during the same time period in different parts of Europe. It reached its maximum increase in Anglo-Saxon England with 33 letters—the original 24 of the

Lindholm Amulet. Bone. 6th century.

On one side are the words: "I am an Herulian, I am called the Cunning One."
The Heruli were a lost tribe fabled for their skill in rune magic, and
"Herulian" was a byword for rune master. On the other side occur a series of
runes (aaaaaaaaRRRnnn?bmuttt) and the magical word (alu) meaning protection. In all there are 24 runes in the series, one being obscured by a frac-
ture. The use of the amulet is not known. It was found in a piece of peat in the
year 1840, by a farm woman just as she was about to put it into a stove and
burn it.

—Reproduced by permission of Lund University, Sweden

futhark with slight modifications, plus nine new runes. It was reduced most strikingly in Scandinavia to only 16 letters.

Through all these changes the alphabet retained its basic structure. The Germans had divided it into three parts, called *aettir*, each containing eight runes in a fixed order. The word *aettir* is from the Old Norse and means families or generations. Each *aett* was named for the rune that began it. In Old English, the first is called Feoh (ᚠ), the second Haegl (ᚺ) and the third Tyr (ᛏ). In the Norse runes, the *aettir* have been reduced to six, five and five letters respectively but they have retained their names and underlying form; a remarkable survival that indicates the importance of these divisions.

It is often pointed out that on the Lindholm amulet, a small curved wand of animal bone, the rune ᚨ (Os) occurs eight times in succession, and the runes ᚣ (Eolh), ᛁ (Is) and ᛏ (Tyr) are each repeated three times, in a line that contains a total of 24 runes. Similar series elsewhere lead scholars to speculate on the hidden significance of numbers in Teutonic magic, but as this is a very obscure subject to most archaeologists and historians, they have little to say.

As Christianity extended its sway over Europe, it carried with it the Latin language and the priests to teach it. Runes never became a common medium for writing. They were used as decorations and occasionally as the subject around which to construct riddles. Only in the far north did they become cursive— so simplified they could be quickly jotted down. Cursive rune writing is like shorthand and is unintelligible to the untrained eye. Meaning is dependent on the relationship of the marks to the lines that border them:

Halsinge cursive:

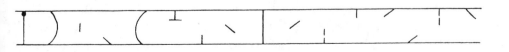

Germanic equivalents:

ᚠᚢᚦᚨ ᚱ ᚲ ᚺᚾ ᛁ ᛊ ᛦᛋᛏᛒᛗ ᛚ

The Church abhorred the magical use of runes by the recently converted peoples who came under its wing. Priests sought to discourage such activity for more pragmatic reasons—they wished to be the only dispensers of charms and incantations. Sometimes the oppression was heavy, and sometimes it was light. The early Church, uncertain of its power, had to tread softly around the hereditary beliefs of recently pagan kings.

Pope Gregory, a remarkably shrewd man, ordered his missionary priests not to suppress the elements of pagan worship but to absorb them into the body of Christianity. In 601 A.D. he writes:

> I have come to the conclusion that the idols among the people should on no account be destroyed, but the temples asperged with holy water, altars set up in them and relics deposited there . . . In this way, we hope that the people, seeing their temples are not destroyed, may abandon their error and flocking more readily to their accustomed resorts may come to know and adore the true God.

Such moderation on the part of the Christian fathers was rare indeed. As the power of the Church increased, so did its despotism. The last significant use of runes occurred in Iceland, that outpost of the Viking Empire, where as late as 1639 it was deemed necessary to officially prohibit the use of runes. But by this time in Europe, runes were already dead. They turned up occasionally in old church manuscripts penned by Gothic monks, who had used them as a form of scholarly recreation.

It is ironic that the main source of information about the runes are the manuscript libraries of the very institution that insured that runes should perish as a force in human culture. The Church had succeeded in doing to the runes what it does best. It obliterated them. Gone are the techniques for applying runes to life situations. Gone are the all-important chants which

Derbyshire Bone Piece. Bone. 8th century.
The runes perpetuate the name of their inscriber, Hodda. This fragment is perhaps part of a comb or comb case.

empowered them and made them function.

All that survive are a few pathetic folk charms. References in the heroic sagas of the Norsemen where occasional hints are given as to the use and power of runes. A scattering of historical references. Monuments erected long after the magical use of runes was forgotten. A few riddling rune poems. A small number of artifacts discovered in burial mounds and under bodies of water where they had rested the centuries undisturbed. When you have studied these fragments, you have all that remains of rune lore.

Far from being a discouragement, this should provide a challenge to the modern student who has on his side the magical methods of the past and a knowledge of symbolism to help him reconstruct from these hints the full glory of rune magic. Runes operate according to the universal laws of magic. A skilled Magus can reconstruct from his own practical experience the ritual methods the Teutonic pagans probably used. More importantly, he can create a fully functional system of rune magic that is effective in the present day.

Chapter 3

ANCIENT MAGICAL USES OF RUNES

The Roman historian Tacitus in the year 98 A.D. makes reference to divination by runes in his work *Germania.* He writes:

> Augury and divination by lot no people practice more diligently. The use of the lots is simple. A little bough is lopped off a fruit-bearing tree and cut into small pieces; these are destinguished by certain marks and thrown carelessly and at random over a white cloth. In public questions the priest of the particular state—in private the father of the family—invokes the gods and with his eyes toward heaven takes up three pieces one at a time and finds in them a meaning according to the marks previously impressed on them.

It is unlikely Tacitus ever saw this form of divination firsthand. There was much travel to the far outposts of the Roman Empire in his day, and like all good historians he made a habit of collecting travelers' tales. The Romans were obsessed with auguries of all kinds. Tacitus, a popular writer, is careful to mention that aspect of runes most likely to interest his readers.

A more highly colored impression is given by the poet of the *Andreas,* an Old English poem:

29

> Casting lots they let them decree
> Which should die first as food for the others.
> With hellish acts and heathen rites
> They cast the lots and counted them out.

The writer was a Christian whose prime concern was in poisoning the reputation of pagans, so his statements should not be taken too seriously.

In the *Voluspa* edda and in *Beowulf*, mention is made of divination, probably by runes, and the venerable Bede states that casting lots was customary among the ancient Saxons. Unfortunately, only Tacitus has given a detailed description of the method, and that a very brief account.

Runes also played an active role in magic. In the right hands, they could make things happen. Bede describes how in 679 a Northumbrian captive named Imma whose fetters kept falling off was asked by his captors: "whether he knew loosening runes and had about him the letters written down." Imma may have used the charm spoken of by Odin through the mouth of the composer of the *Havamal*:

> I know a fourth (charm),
> which frees me quickly,
> if foes should bind me fast,
> a chant I know
> that breaks fetters,
> bursts bonds.

Amulet Ring. 9th century.
The use of this and similar rings in the British Museum collection is unknown, but it is most likely avertive.

The eddic *Sigrdrifumal* lists the classes of victory runes, protection runes, birth runes, surf runes, health runes, speech runes and thought runes. Runes were also used for inducing love and making the dead speak. Runic inscriptions have been found inside barrow mounds, where presumably only the dead could read them.

The most prominent magical use of runes seems to have been connected with battle. There were spells to blunt the swords of the enemy, to make a warrior invisible, to sap the battle will of a foe, to insure that a man not be slain in war.

Runes were cut on the sides of weapons and inlaid in gold wire, or colored with red pigment. A sword found on the Isle of Wight bears the magical name Increase to Pain, or the motto: Woe to the weapons of the foe. Names of power were not uncommon on weapons. A spearhead of the third century is called Tester. Another bears the name Attacker. That these are magical names cannot be doubted. Sometimes the runic inscriptions are intermingled with more ancient Stone-Age signs—the pre-runic rock carvings from which the magical function of runes evolved.

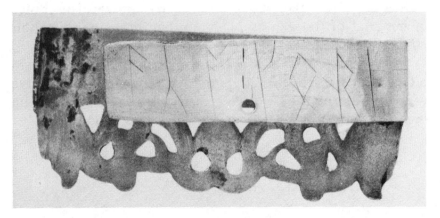

Chessel Down Sword Hilt. Iron. Isle of Wight, 7th or 8th century.
On the inner side of the silver scabbard-mount occur the runes (aeco: soeri) which have been interpreted: "Woe to the weapons (of the foe)" but more correctly should read: "increase—sorrow (pain)." This is clearly the name of the sword, a magical inscription to add to its might.

Runes were also inscribed on defensive war gear. A third century helmet from Negau bears the German words in a North Italic script: "to the god Herigast." The intention is clear. The soldier who wore the helmet hoped that Herigast would not allow a thing consecrated in his name to be shattered by an axe. Shields were painted with the Tyr (↑) rune to infuse them with the war spirit of Tiw, the Teutonic Mars. The rune Ψ (Eolh) was also used singly as a charm to ward off evil, as were the magical words *alu* (taboo) and *laukaz* (leek). The houseleek plant retained its avertive associations down into the Middle Ages, when it was planted on cottage roofs all over Europe to ward off lightning, fire and witches.

More interesting from a magical viewpoint are the rune wands—short staffs of yew or bone inscribed with runes for occult purposes. They have flattened sides and are sometimes curved and tapered like horns. The most beautiful example is the Lindholm amulet (page 24), a minor work of art, but often they are fairly crude. The Britsum amulet bears the message "always carry this yew in the host of battle." The yew tree was sacred to the Celts and was widely believed to attract magical influences. Yew bows were prized for their power. The choice of material of the wands played a significant part in their efficacy.

In addition to help in winning the battle, the Norsemen often needed aid to reach it. More feared than the enemy were winter storms on the North Sea. Surf runes were used to calm the waves and still the winds. In the *Havamal* Odin says:

> I know a ninth (charm)—
> when need of it.
> to shelter my ship from winter storm,
> the wind it calms,
> the waves abate,
> the sea is put to sleep.

In the *Volsunga* the former Valkyrie Brynhild says to the warrior Sigurd:

> Sea-runes good at need,
> Learnt for ship's saving,
> For the good health of the swimming horse;

On the stern cut them,
Cut them on the rudder-blade
And set flame to shaven oar:
Howso big be the sea-hills
Howso blue beneath,
Hail from the main then comest thou home.

It is probable that the charm involved carving runes on one of the rudder oars after it had been shaved with an axe into splinters to make it kindle, then setting fire to it with a spoken invocation to the appropriate god—perhaps Thor, who fought the Midgard serpent. A sacrifice of blood would be made on the runes before they were burned.

The power of runes over the elements was not confined to the sea. Storms could be summoned or stilled over land as well by means of weather runes. The Teutons considered suspect all sudden onslaughts of snow, hail and wind.

Another charm against the elements that would fall into the category of taboo runes is one against fire. Odin says:

I know a seventh charm—
if a hall blazes around
my bench mates,
though hot the flames,
they feel nought.

This would be not so much a personal charm as a protection for members of the household. The verse implies that the warriors in the hall could go on eating and drinking while the walls crackled around them. Protection from fire is a common feature of magic found in diverse cultures around the world.

Encounters in the mead hall were not always friendly. The Vikings were not above using poison when it suited their purpose. Special runes could be cut in the rim of a drinking horn, into the backs of the hands, and on the fingernails to warn of its presence in the cup. The rune ᚾ (Nyd) is mentioned specifically. Also mentioned is the magic word *laukaz*.

In *Egil's Saga*, the rune master Egil Skalla-Grimsson suspects poison in his drinking horn. He scratches runes on the vessel and stains them with his blood, then chants an evocatory verse over them. In the words of the poet: "The horn sprang asunder, and the drink spilt down into the straw."

Egil played the lead role in another magic episode when he came across a charm that someone unskilled in rune lore had placed in the bed of a sick woman. Ten runes had been cut on a piece of whalebone. According to Egil, this had actually extended the sickness. After removing the charm Egil cut runes of his own and put them under the mattress of the sick bed. The woman awoke as out of a deep sleep and said that she was healed.

Egil gives this solemn warning to those who would dabble in rune lore without understanding the craft:

> Runes shall a man not score,
> Save he can well to read them.
> That many a man betideth,
> On a mirk stave to stumble.

Not everyone willing to use magical methods understood them. Certain tribes were renowed for rune craft more than others. The Heruli were especially celebrated for magical learning. Driven out of Denmark by the Danes, they spread to various parts of Europe and carried the runes with them. Long after they had vanished as a people, the term Herulian continued to connote a sage skilled in runes. See the Lindholm amulet, page 24.

Women were not excluded in Teutonic cultures. They could own property and control events. There were female warriors, at least in myth, and female wizards in real life equivalent to the rural wise women of recent times. One such rune-witch is described in *Eric the Red's Saga*, a seeress named Thorbjorg who was often consulted about the future:

> She was wearing a blue cloak with straps which was set with stones right down to the hem; she had glass beads about her neck, and on her head a black lambskin hood lined inside with white catskin. She had a staff in her hand, with a knob on it; it was ornamented with brass and set around with stones just below the knob. Round her middle she wore a belt made of touchwood, and on it was a big pouch in which she kept those charms of hers which she needed for her magic. On her feet she had hairy calf-skin shoes with long

> thongs, and on the thong ends big knobs of lateen. She
> had on her hands catskin gloves which were white
> inside and hairy.

A more malevolent witch named Duridr is spoken of in
Grettis Saga. To bring disaster onto Grettir, the witch cuts runes
into the root of a tree, then reddens them with her blood while
chanting a spell of doom. The staining of runes, usually with
blood, seems an integral factor in their functioning. The Old
English root word for pigment, specifically red ochre, is related
to the Old Norse root for sorcery.

More benevolent wise women would have been much
sought after during difficult childbirths. There is a runic charm
to ease delivery mentioned in the *Volsunga Saga*:

> Help-runes shalt thou gather
> If skill thou wouldst gain
> To loosen child from low-laid mother;
> Cut be they in the hands hollow,
> Wrapped the joints round about;
> Call for the Good-folks' gainsome helping.

Presumably the runes were to be cut into the palms of the
mother. Again, blood is significant in the working of the magic.
The Good-folk may have been fairies.

For wounds this advice is given:

> Learn the bough-runes wisdom
> If leech thou lovest;
> And wilt wot about wounds' searching
> On the bark be they scored;
> On the buds of trees
> Whose boughs look eastward ever.

All the above uses of runes are to combat natural circumstances. There is a class of rune magic designed to deal with
supernatural forces. One rune charm turns a magical attack back
on its sender. Says Odin in the *Havamal*:

> if runes are cut to harm me,
> the spell is turned,
> the hunger harmed,
> not I.

Another banishes obsessing spirits by making it impossible

for the spirits to put on a form or find a resting place:

> if spirits trouble,
> I work, they wander afar,
> unable to find form or home.

Runes could open for their master the highest, but also the lowest, domains of magic. To the latter belong works of necromancy, the art of animating the dead. This is sometimes thought to involve calling back into the corpse the soul of the person it once contained, but such is not the case. The corpse merely acts as a material vessel for a spirit in order that the spirit may pass on the information the sorcerer requires:

> when I see aloft a tree
> a corpse swinging from a rope,
> then I cut and paint runes,
> so the man walks,
> and speaks with me.

In most cases the necromancers did not understand the distinction between calling back from death the soul of a human being and evoking a spirit in the flesh of the corpse. Since the spirit often lied to the necromancer and claimed to be the dead man's ghost, the necromancer had little reason to revise his opinion.

In a deceptively lighter vein, rune magic could be used to overcome the modesty of a maiden and cause her to submit to the advances of a man, or could make a young man infatuated with an older woman. Love magic is often trivialized. In fact, it is a crime of the blackest kind to warp the perceptions of another human being and cause that person to love what was formerly loathed.

Fortunately, love charms are most used where none are needed, between lovers, and then their effects are inconsequential. The herbal portion of such charms was put in beer or mead, a wine made of honey. In the *Volsunga Saga* "Brynhild filled a beaker and bore it to Sigurd, and gave him the drink of love." She says:

> Mixed is it mightily,
> Mingled with fame,
> Brimming with bright lays
> And pitiful runes,

A large class of rune magic dealt with what are called word runes and thought runes. Word runes gave their possessor a ready tongue at the *thing*—the tribal council where legal matters were decided. If the rune master had wronged another man he might hope to escape just punishment (usually a fine of gold or cattle) by pleading his case so eloquently that no listener would find in his accuser's favor. A glib and clever tongue was a characteristic of the god Odin. In the *Volsunga* Brynhild says:

> Word-runes learn well
> If thou wilt that no man
> Pay back grief for the grief thou gavest;
> Wind thou these,
> Weave thou these,
> Cast thou these all about thee,
> At the Thing,
> Where folk throng,
> Unto the full doom faring.

Associated with word runes but of a deeper significance are the thought runes. These enable their bearer to hear and understand the inspired wisdom of the gods. Brynhild says:

> Thought-runes shalt thou deal with
> If thou wilt be of all men
> Fairest-souled wight, and wisest,

This is sharply different in tone from the somewhat cynical description of word runes. Thought runes not only granted material knowledge, but spiritual wisdom as well. They make the soul white by washing away sin. Thought runes would be mainly sought after by priests and magicians of the higher order, who were less concerned with things of the body and more involved in matters of the spirit. They are avenues for the communication of the Higher Self with the ego.

This refutes the assertations of some scholars that runes are completely materialistic. The poet T. S. Eliot wrote: "Runes and charms are very practical formulae designed to produce definite results, such as getting a cow out of a bog."

The statement is true as far as it goes, but it encourages a distorted understanding of runes. The Teutonic peoples faced enormous hardships both from nature and from their fierce human foes. Their primary concern was physical survival, and rune lore reflects this preoccupation; but to assume from this that no one using the runes was capable of more refined philosophical and theological aspirations is unjustified. Merely because such thoughts were never written down does not mean they never existed.

The use of runes to achieve spiritual growth is no less a practical matter than getting a cow out of a bog. Those who believe what they cannot see is in some way impractical, and by inference not worth bothering about, betray their ignorance. Scholars often fail to perceive the higher aspects of rune magic because they are blind to the light of Spirit. They assiduously sift through the empty husks of rune lore but miss the kernels of wisdom that lie scattered all around them.

A minor use of runes but one worth mentioning is the induction of sleep. Odin, angered by Brynhild's betrayal of his will, caused her to enter a magical sleep. According to Brynhild, he "stuck the sleep-thorn" into her. The Thorn (Þ) is a rune, but whether it had any part in Odin's spell is moot. The German fairy tale of Sleeping Beauty, who was surrounded by a wall of thorns, may relate to this legend. There are many such correspondences between German folk tales and Teutonic mythology. A charm in the *Havamal* may be a riddle for this magical sleep:

> The first charm I know
> is unknown to all
> of any human kind,
> 'Help' it is named,
> for help it gives,
> in hours of anguish,
> and in sorrow.

That there were countless other uses to which runes were put can be inferred from the diversity of examples that have come down through history. Rune magic was not a rigid formula but a flexible tool that could be freely applied by a master of runes to any problem in life.

Since runes are a tool without moral strictures attached to

them, they could be and were used as readily for evil as for good. When evilly employed, they exacted a payment in evil. When used for good, they conveyed an increase of good. In knowing hands they provided the means for exhalting the human soul to its highest level. They truly are the legacy of Odin to his people:

> Some abide with the Elves,
> Some abide with the Aesir,
> Or with the wise Vanir,
> Some still hold the sons of mankind.

> These be the book-runes
> And the runes of good help,
> And all the taboo-runes
> And the runes of much might;
> To whomso they may avail
> Unbewildered, unspoilt;
> They are wholesome to have:
> Thrive thou with these then,
> When thou hast learnt their lore,
> Til the Gods end thy life-days.

Frank's Casket—Front. Whalebone. Northumbria, 8th century.
The left panel shows Weland the Smith standing over the headless body of one of King Nithhad's sons, holding a cup made of the slain man's skull. On the right side Weland's brother Egil strangles birds from whose feathers he made wings that allowed Weland to escape Nithhad's captivity.

The right panel depicts the Christian scene of the adoration of the Magi. The runes *magi* are carved over the figures of the wise men. The runes around the edge tell of the beached whale from whose bones the casket was made.

Frank's Casket—Left side. Whalebone. Northumbria, 8th century.
A scene showing the suckling of Romulus and Remus, mythical founders of Rome, by a wolf. The runes describe the scene.

Chapter 4

MEANING OF THE RUNES

Below is the German *futhark* of 24 characters, the first settled form of runes. Wiccan and other pagan groups sometimes use the 28 or 33 character Anglo-Saxon rune alphabet, called *futhorc* because of the altered pronunciation of the first six letters. Additions to the original runes will be dealt with later.

The primary form of each rune is followed by its secondary forms (if any) its name, the short meaning of the name, and its transliteration. Old English names for the runes are used because they are easier to pronounce and to remember, but it should be borne in mind that the runes are German. After the summary, a detailed examination is made into the levels of meaning of each rune and possible ways it can be used magically.

1.   FEOH (Cattle) — f

Feoh begins and names the first of the three *aettir*. The beast of burden and by association the qualities that characterize cattle.

	German *futhark*	Anglo-Saxon *futhorc*	
		1st addition	2nd addition
ᛚ	ᚠ FEOH (Cattle)-f ᚢ UR (Aurochs)-u ᚦ THORN (Devil) -th ᚩ OS (God)-a ᚱ RAD (Riding)-r ᚲ KEN (Torch)-k ᚷ GYFU (Gift)-g ᚹ WYN (Glory)-w	ᚪ AC (Oak)-a ᚫ AESC (Ash)-ae ᚣ YR (Saddle)-y ᛠ EAR (Earth)-ea	ᛡ IOR (Eel)-io _ ᛣ CALC (Cup)-k̄ ᚸ GAR (Spear)-ḡ ᛢ CWEORD (-)-q ᛥ STAN (Stone) -st
ᚺ	ᚻ HAEGL (Hail) -h ᚾ NYD (Need)-n ᛁ IS (Ice)-i ᛃ GER (Harvest) -j ᛇ EOH (Yew)-ei ᛈ PEORD (Apple) -p ᛉ EOLH (De- fense)-z ᛋ SIGEL (Sun)-s		
ᛏ	ᛏ TYR (Tiw)-t ᛒ BEORC (Birch) -b ᛖ EH (Horse)-e ᛗ MAN (Man)-m ᛚ LAGU (Water) -l ᛝ ING (Fertility god)-ng ᛞ DAEG (Day)-d ᛟ ETHEL (Home- land)-o		

That which is domestic and mild. Of a broken spirit. Slavish, stupid, slow. To be used and owned by free men. Cowardly. The shape of the rune is like the horned head of a cow.

Since cattle are movable possessions and were used in Germany to pay debts, the early meaning was submerged by the concept of wealth. There were no ambivalent feelings about riches in the days prior to Christianity. Feoh was looked upon as a completely positive rune. It was associated not merely with possession but with honor as well. Great wealth enabled a man to make rich presents which won him much renown. For this reason the Scylding family mentioned in *Beowolf* was held in high regard.

The notion of Feoh may at one time have included human cattle, or slaves, who were looked upon as beasts of burden and units of wealth. To give slaves captured in battle, and later to give the equivalent measure of gold, was to give some of the battle glory to another. A man's courage and strength were measured by his plunder.

Magically, Feoh can be used in a good or evil way. If used to signify that someone has power over his environment or that his wealth will increase, it is beneficial. But if applied directly with scornful intent it increases cowardliness and dullness. It can be used to break the spirit of an enemy and render him incapable of effective action. It can create fear and a fawning dependence.

2. Also ⋀ and ⋀ UR (Aurochs) — u

Aurochs is the name for a species of wild ox that lived in the forests of Europe. It was hunted to extinction in the 17th century. Six feet tall at the shoulder with shaggy black hair and large curling horns, it possessed the fierceness of a wild boar and the strength of a bull. It had much the same meaning for the Teutonic hunters as the American bison for the plains Indians.

Julius Caesar, one of the earliest literate Romans to penetrate the wilderness of Germany, gives a good account of this beast in his *Gallic Wars*:

> . . . an animal somewhat smaller than an elephant
> with the appearance, color and shape of a bull. They
> are very strong and agile, and attack every man and
> beast they catch sight of. The natives take great pains
> to trap them in pits, and then kill them. This arduous
> sport toughens the young men and keeps them in
> training; and those who kill the largest number exhibit
> the horns in public to show what they have done, and
> earn high praise. It is impossible to domesticate or
> tame the aurochs, even if caught young. The horns are
> much larger than those of our oxen and of quite dif-
> ferent shape and appearance. The Germans prize
> them greatly; they mount the rims with silver and use
> them as drinking-cups at their grandest banquets.

When the qualities of the animal are abstracted it can be perceived that Ur meant an elemental masculine potency. Physically: strength, agility and endurance. Emotionally: courage and boldness. Spiritually: freedom. Thus, that which can never be domesticated or enslaved. The triumphant soul of nature. The shape of Ur is a horn or erect phallus.

This meaning is in direct contrast to that of the Feoh rune. Clearly the first two runes form a pair. A similar pattern runs throughout the alphabet and is useful in determining the shades of meaning of obscure runes. The pairs are not always opposites but always present a sharp contrast.

The aurochs was synonymous with manhood. That it had a magical significance is suggested by the costly decoration and careful preservation of its horns, and also by the fact that although aurochs did not extend into Britain in historical times, the Anglo-Saxons retained the beast as emblematic of the rune. Perhaps killing the aurochs was a rite of passage into manhood.

Magically, the Ur rune can be used to send resolve and courage, to restore hope, to galvanize into action. Also to increase sexual potency in men. When applied indirectly it can be used as a threat and a medium of destructive force.

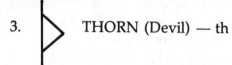

3.   THORN (Devil) — th

In the narrowest sense, Thorn is the name of an evil giant. His figure has survived to the present in the children's fairy tale of Jack and the Beanstalk. It has been translated more generally as Demon.

The shape of the rune is sharp and cutting—like a tooth or claw. This probably led the Anglo-Saxons to change the meaning to the thorn found on rose bushes. Both old and new meanings retain the idea of pain and strife. The *Old English Rune Poem* reads:

> The thorn is extremely sharp, painful
> for any warrior to grasp, immeasurably fierce
> to any man who rests among them.

This seems an exaggerated description to be used by a warrior race accustomed to hardship of all sorts, but when applied to a giant demon, it is appropriate. Although the early meaning of the rune was forgotten, its associations lingered on. The demon Thorn might well be called immeasurably fierce.

In general, the rune conveys a sense of evil force inimical to human will. It is the brute destructive power of Chaos opposed to the world order. All the worst associations of the frost giants apply here. Giants were called "torturers of women" in Scandinavian rune poems, a term summarizing their base cruelty.

Magically, this rune is evil when applied directly to another person. It can be used to call upon them confusion and destruction, to literally visit them with the demon. Used simply to embody evil, it can be fenced around by other protective runes and can play a part in removing evil from an individual or a place afflicted.

4. F Also F OS (God) — a

A god, probably Odin. In an Icelandic poem this rune is glossed "prince of Asgard and lord of Valhalla." In later Anglo-Saxon runes it comes to mean mouth, and in Scandinavian runes, mouth of a river. These later meanings accord well with the nature of Odin, who was the wise god, lord of poetry and cunning speech.

Two stories told about Odin reveal this part of his nature. To gain wisdom, Odin begged his uncle Mimir, a water demon whose name means He who Thinks, to allow him a drink from his fountain where all knowledge and wisdom lay hidden. Mimir agreed on condition that Odin tear out his eye and hand it over as a pledge. So desirous was Odin of obtaining the wisdom of the fountain that he acceded to this condition, and from then on he was known as the One-Eyed.

Not content with wisdom, Odin sought skill in poetry. The giant Suttung possessed the hydromel, a fabulous drink made of blood and honey that caused anyone who sipped even a drop to become a great bard. Through craft and skill, Odin gained the confidence of Suttung's daughter, Gunnlod, who allowed him to sip the hydromel on three separate nights in return for his amorous favors. In three gulps Odin drank all the hydromel and carried it off, gaining sole possession of all poetry, except for a few drops that fell to the ground during his flight.

That which distinguishes man from the beasts is reasoned speech. The God of the Hebrews created the entire world with a Word. In Teutonic mythology life springs from rivers and fountains, which are analogous to the speaking mouth of God as sources of creative energy. Therefore, this rune presents the opposite to the force of Chaos. The personification of reason and law in nature, and the giver of human laws that are in harmony with the will of God. What is kind, benevolent, just. The source of true happiness.

Magically, this is a very favorable rune. It opens the way for judgment into difficult and confusing situations. It brings calm. It carries Light into darkness. In its secondary meaning it gives knowledge and good speech, and acts as an avenue of divine revelation. The biblical prophets may be said to have prophesied under the influence of this rune.

5. 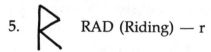 RAD (Riding) — r

A journey on horseback. In the *Old English Rune Poem* the journey is said to be strenuous, the horse powerful, the road long. All three elements are laden with significance. For the ancient Germans, travel where the roads were few and bad was of epic proportions. Moderate journeys required weeks—longer journeys months or even years. Physical endurance was tested to the limit. The journey became a metaphor for life itself.

Complete dependence was placed on the horse. Without it the traveler would be left on foot in the wilderness at the mercy of wolves and other things less natural. The horse became transportation itself, equivalent to the ship at sea. It has been suggested that Rad acted as a charm for travelers. The rune possessed a mystical association with journeying of all kinds. Perhaps it was given to the dead to guide and assist them on their road to the underworld.

In the abstract, Rad means a seeking and striving. A quest. A search for fulfillment, perhaps a search for spiritual wisdom. On the material level: physical travel, change in address, forced relocation.

Magically, it can be used to seek into the unknown. Applied to another person, it arouses restlessness and dissatisfaction, and causes changes in life that may be good or bad depending on which runes accompany it.

6.   ᚲ   Also ᚴ KEN (Torch) — k

Originally referred to light, which in ancient times was provided by torches and fires. Human light as opposed to the natural light of the sun. The physical light of flame was easily associated with the light of the mind, just as darkness is linked with ignorance. The piercing keenness of the intellect lights the dark places of the soul and dispels shadows. The rune may have become linked with the passage of the dead. The rider on the long road to the underworld carried Ken, the illuminating light of his reason, as a guide and comfort.

The highest virtues have always been associated with radiance. There are references in the gospels to the shining light of Christ. Revelations from God to the prophets took the form of light—as when Moses saw the burning bush. White is a sacred color in diverse cultures. The white buffalo of the American Indians. The white knight of European folklore. The white dove of peace.

In the Cynewulfin signatures, passages where the Anglo-Saxon poet placed his name in the form of rune riddles, Ken is used as a cipher for intelligence. Speaking of the final judgment, Cynwulf says: "Then *cin* will tremble, will hear the King, the Ruler of heaven, speak, pronounce stern words to those who obeyed him negligently before in the world." This would seem to be light used as the gift of the personal self—the soul—from God.

The early Germans burned their dead. Attempts have been made to link the Ken rune with some rite of a sun cult. Symbols of the sun figure prominently in the Stone Age rock carvings and appear beside runes on some weapon relics—the spearhead found near Brestlitovsk in the USSR, for example. Such a connection would not be incompatible with the interpretation of Ken as progressively torch, light and intelligence.

The Scottish word *ken* which now means to know, but which earlier meant to see, to recognize, and was also used to indicate the range of vision or sight, may be a descendant of the Ken rune. The shape of the rune is of something that flies and pierces.

Magically, the rune can be used in conjunction with its partner Rad to penetrate mysteries. Applied to another directly it dispels ignorance and brings about sudden realizations and insights. Perversely applied it frustrates learning. It represents the highest of the three levels of man.

7.   ✕   GYFU (Gift) — g

Gifts played an important part in German culture. A chief would support the young warriors who followed him with gifts of horses, weapons and lavish feasts. Relations between tribes were always conducted with the exchange of costly presents. Tacitus writes in his *Germania*:

> It is usual to give the departing guest whatever he may ask for, and a present in return is asked with as little hesitation. They are greatly charmed with gifts, but they expect no return for what they give, nor feel any obligation for what they receive.

The giving to, and receiving of gifts from, the gods would have been looked upon as a natural extension of these customs. Accordingly, Gyfu has been regarded as a magical symbol connected with sacrifice. It seems probable that it refers more to sacrifices made to the gods than gifts of the gods to men because of the nature of Teutonic deities—the pagan gods such as Thor and Odin could be expected to gift a man only with strength and cunning. Even this might be capriciously withdrawn on a whim. On the other hand, men were obligated to sacrifice to the gods lest the gods become angry and visit them with misfortunes.

Even before the advent of Christianity, it would be reasonable to link Gyfu with charity. Generosity was the virtue of great chiefs. The covetous were despised and believed to suffer an ill fate. Gyfu would generally mean something of personal value, freely and willingly given away. It might be a life sacrifice— forsaking present happiness for future joy. It is good to sacrifice the lower for the higher; evil to sacrifice the higher for the lower. The cross is an ancient symbol of suffering.

Magically, a sign of initiation. What must be given up in order to gain wisdom and spiritual power. No advance is possible without pain and loss. The rune can be applied to another person favorably as the bringer of gifts, or unfavorably as the causer of sacrifice.

8. 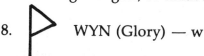 WYN (Glory) — w

Usually translated as joy, a better meaning is glory because it suggests pleasure in possession. Glory is an intangible thing, yet it can be gained or lost. While it is possessed it is displayed as a badge of honor. Glory encompasses joy, in that no glorying is possible without joy.

In relation to its paired complement Gyfu, Wyn is what results from gift giving. It is the natural reward for sacrifice. Sacrifice to the gods is repaid with success in battle and honor in life. Generosity brings all manner of rewards both tangible and spiritual. In the highest form Wyn is ecstasy, a merging with the divine Light.

Odin is mentioned in connection with this rune in an Anglo-Saxon poem, the *Nine Herbs Charm*:

> For Woden took nine glory-twigs,
> he smote then the adder that it flew apart into nine
> parts.

The adder is the serpent in the Garden of Eden, a diminished form of dragon. The glory twigs are magic wands with runes cut into them representing nine natural forces. However, cutting anything with nine objects results in ten parts. Nine was used symbolically in the poem as a cycle of perfection, a trine of trinities. The number ten begins a new cycle and is therefore tangible. Smiting the serpent is implied as a spiritual act.

Magically, Wyn is a reward for spiritual sacrifice; the force flickering in the name given to the neophyte when he takes on his magical identity and is exhalted above the common man. The rune can be used as a vessel of energy in the same way Odin used it, to project authority. Glory in the eyes of the gods translates as strength in dealings with men.

9.   ᚺ   Also ᚻ and ᛨ   HAEGL (Hail) — h

Haegl can be literally interpreted as hail, a miraculous and terrifying phenomenon of nature. It must have seemed to the Teutons that the gods were venting their wrath on the earth when they threw down white stones to blight crops and kill fowl. Hail was thought to be one of the weapons of the frost giants.

In the abstract, Haegl means hardship. Involuntary suffering without reason. The afflictions of Job. Any injustice thrust upon a man by the fates. The loss of a loved one. An inexplicable sickness. The sinking of a ship or the laming of a horse. Disaster of a violent nature. Haegl is an active and masculine destroyer. It beats down a field of grain with hammer strokes. Its action is visible and physical.

This rune begins the second *aett* which bears its name. It has been speculated that Haegl is the name of an unknown god since the runes that begin the other two *aettir* can be connected with two gods: Feoh is a natural symbol for Frey, and Tyr is another name for Tiw. Since no reference to a god Haegl has ever been found, this is only speculation. If Haegl is a god he may have filled a role similar to the Hindu goddess Kali, the Destroyer. Tiw is a god of judicial mediation. Frey is a god of generation. The trinity would be rounded by a god of destruction.

Magically, Haegl is a rune that lends itself to evil use. To project its quality on another is to send them suffering and hardship, which may be more precisely defined by the runes that accompany it. This is suffering without hope of redemption, remorseless pain and loss of a violent kind.

10.　　Ⓧ　　NYD (Need) — n

The necessity to endure. That element in the human spirit which will not allow it to accept its fate. Stubborn will to resist even when there is no hope. Resistance against all odds. It shows itself in circumstances of extreme trial such as deathly sickness or natural disaster: the cancer patient who refuses to accept death; the accident victim who continues to fight through icy waters after his consciousness has deserted him—these people illustrate the power of Nyd.

There is no glory in Nyd. It is described in the poem *Solomon and Saturn* as the worst lot that can befall a man. No credit arises from exhibiting resistance to such supreme hardship because it lies beyond the level of willful control. Nyd is sent by the gods to test and to teach. It produces a tempering of the spirit. One who experiences Nyd and lives is the stronger for it. In historical times, the death camps of Nazi Germany generated large amounts of Nyd.

Nyd is linked with Haegl in several ancient references. In the *Abecedarium Nordmannicum* the two runes occur on the same line, which reads: "hail has need." In the *Old English Rune Poem* the verses for Haegl and Nyd have parallel constructions:

> Hail is the whitest of grains; it whirls down from
>   heaven's height,
> and gusts of wind toss it about; then it is transformed
>   to water.

> Hardship oppresses the heart; yet nonetheless often it
>   is transformed for the sons of men
> to a source of help and salvation, if only they heed
>   it in time.

Nyd is the power in the human spirit that allows it to endure Haegl. The two go together. Without great hardship the necessity to endure would never be exercised. The shape of the Nyd rune suggests a broken cross, or perhaps a man carrying an awkward and unbalanced load.

Magically, the rune carries fortitude and defiance when all hope has been lost. It gives fearlessness in the face of certain death. Cast on another it can provide the inner strength to allow them to survive extreme sufferings of a physical or psychological kind. But cast indirectly with negative intent, it carries hardship.

11. | IS (Ice) — i

In the narrow sense this rune stands for ice, particularly the flat floor or bridge of ice that covers inlets of the sea, lakes and rivers. All northern races used ice for highways in winter. Such roads had their treacherous aspect. An unwary traveler might fall through and be lost without a trace. In the *Icelandic Rune Poem* is written:

> Ice is bark of rivers
> and roof of the wave
> and destruction for doomed men.

The qualities that distinguish ice are stealth and treachery. It forms silently, sealing up open waters in a steel-like case. It is hard when a man might wish it to be soft, and soft when he most wants it to be hard. Never is it to be trusted. It surrounds the hull of a ship and crushes it in savage jaws. It waits for the unwary step and throws down the horse or walking man.

Its deceptive qualities make it feminine. If Haegl is compared to the stroke of an axe, Is is poison in the winecup. Ice has its alluring, seductive aspects. As the *Old English Rune Poem* states:

> it glitters clear as glass, very like jewels;
> it is a floor wrought by the frost, fair to behold.

Much of its danger lies in its inviting appearance. The silence and stillness of ice put the traveler off his guard. One step leads to another, and before he knows it he is in over his head.

Another quality of ice is its changelessness. It locks life under its surface and keeps it motionless as though under a spell. Even the restless waves are stilled. Waterfalls and fountains become rigid monuments to the power of Is.

Magically, it prevents actions through hidden and subtle means. Can be used to freeze an intention or emotion before it is fully developed. Can also cause sudden and unforeseen catastrophe which the victim cannot perceive developing. But its main use is to forestall events.

12.    Also   GER (Harvest) — j

Harvest is the specific meaning of this rune, but for general purposes, cycle may be more useful. It indicates the coming full circle of the year when the labor in the fields during spring and summer is repaid in autumn. The ancient Germans did not recognize autumn as a season. According to Tacitus, they acknowledged only spring, summer and winter. Perhaps they regarded autumn as a summing up of the entire year, rather than as a separate and equal quarter.

Generalized Ger is any revolution or cycle of change. A change of luck. A cycle of life. All natural cycles such as the phases of the moon. The change of the seasons. Ger has variously been defined by scholars as year, spring, summer and harvest season. Its broader meaning encompasses all these.

For the Teutons, the most obvious cycle was the change from winter to summer, and from summer to winter. The joys and plenties of the harvest are opposed to the silent hardship signaled by the freezing over of the lakes, rivers and ocean. The stillness of Is is in sharp contrast to the cyclic motion of Ger. In winter everything stops; with the return of the sun, things begin to move once again. Ger is change, and change is always cyclical.

Even the shape of Ger suggests this whirling energy. It is a tourbillion, a vortex of active forces. The alternate form of Ger shows an axis through the center of a circle. This is a Hindu symbol for generation.

Magically, Ger is used to bring about an inversion of circumstance. It revolves the wheel of fortune and makes the high to be low and the low to be high. It causes events to come full circle. More esoterically, it is used to actualize desire by making inner vision into physical reality. The fruition of designs.

13.   EOH (Yew) — ei (a sound between e and i)

The yew is an evergreen tree with bright red berries and a very durable, elastic wood. It was used to make bows, and one of the translations of Eoh is bow made of yew. Yew bows were greatly prized for their strength.

It also seems to have been related to burning. The *Norwegian Rune Poem* reads:

> Yew is the greenest of trees in winter;
> when it burns, it sputters.

In the *Old English Rune Poem*, Eoh is called a keeper of flame. Fire was sacred to the Teutons. The evergreen color of the yew may have endowed its wood with revitalizing powers. In early times it was customary to burn the bodies of the dead before interring them. Yew rune wands may have been burned on funeral pyres to help the dead attain eternal life.

Yew trees were also planted in cemeteries where they can still be seen today; or perhaps the dead were buried in groves of yew. The yew is thought to draw in supernatural influences. Ancient yews are looked upon with dread. They are thought to absorb and trap the spirits of the dead and keep them from wandering.

A wood that sputters when it burns is not the most desirable for utilitarian use, but in magic the sputter may have been looked upon as a favorable omen. There is a classical form of divination wherein the crackle of laurel boughs cast on a fire is regarded as a good sign.

The wand-shaped amulets found by archaeologists are made of yew wood, attesting that the yew was considered to have magical power of a vitalizing and protective nature. The Eoh rune may be said to signify dependability, strength and vitality. The term yeoman, which originally meant the follower of a chief—a bowman—carries connotations of all these virtues in the phrase "yeoman service."

Magically, this rune is used to lend strength and provide a firm foundation. It is to be relied on in time of need. It can protect a person from himself by rendering him sensible and thoughtful. It guards against self-destructive behavior. More mystically it provides a staff of comfort and help in the darkness of the soul.

14. ᛈ   PEORD (Apple) — p

The original meaning of this rune was probably apple tree. However Peord is one of the more obscure runes and no interpretation is certain. Various definitions have been proposed including pawn, chessman, dice box, table-game, and even penis. These speculations arise from the context of Peord in the *Old English Rune Poem*:

> A table-game (?) is always a source of recreation
>   and amusement
> to proud princes, where warriors sit
> happily together in the mead-hall.

The definition of Peord as some form of game or gaming implement, even if generally correct in the context of the poem, is far removed from its first meaning. All runes once stood for natural objects or elemental forces. It was only when the runes were interpreted by settled societies that they became trivialized. For example, yew became yew-bow; cattle became wealth; the necessity to endure became feudal obligation.

However, if table-game is the degenerate meaning, a link may be formed with the first meaning of the rune—apple tree. Tacitus in his *Germania* mentions that the Germans divined by cutting twigs from a fruit-bearing tree and carving runes on them. The most obvious fruit tree of the northern forests is the apple. History teaches that traditional forms of divination frequently degenerate into games of gambling. The Tarot devolved into common playing cards. Geomancy became dice. It is not unlikely that Germanic divination was reduced over time to a form of table sport—probably some form of draughts. If so, the runic name for the wood used in divination may have carried down to the game.

All this is highly speculative. It is worth noting, however, that a scholar named Marstrander arrived at the same meaning for Peord through a separate philological route. He related the rune name Peord to the Irish name for apple tree, *ceirt*, and connected the two with reference to the evolution of words.

A separate rune for the apple tree makes good sense. There are many tree runes. The apple has powerful magical and mythological associations: the apples of the Tree of Knowledge; the golden apple given to Venus by Paris; the apples of Idun by which the gods preserved their youth; the apples of Sodam, lovely to look upon, but ashes inside; the apples of Istkahor, sweet on one side and bitter on the other.

In Teutonic mythology, the apple seems to have been a beneficent symbol. The phrase "an apple a day keeps the doctor away" is still popular. However, apples are not without their ambivalent aspect. A fruit so luscious and seductive easily becomes a tool for evil. In the fairy tale Snow White, the wicked queen uses an apple to disguise her poison.

For the early Germans, Peord probably signified a Cornucopia of life and health. The shape is enclosing, like a cup tipped on its side. The apple was a pleasurable source of sustenance and therefore to be celebrated in Bacchanalian feasts. The negative connotations derive from the positive—too much celebration brings sickness the morning after. In this sense Peord is opposed to its paired complement Eoh, which is staid and frugal by nature. Both are tree runes, but of markedly different associations. In the fable of the Ant and the Grasshopper, Eoh might stand for the sign of the ant, and Peord for the sign of the grasshopper. Those who exude large amounts of Peord are fun to be around but undependable.

Magically, the rune serves to bring abundance and pleasure even to the point of excess, and is not to be overused. The gayest and brightest of the runes. Cast with evil intent it can seduce others to excesses in gluttony, lust and drunkenness. It can make them spendthrift. Like wine it is delightful in moderation, but deadly in excess.

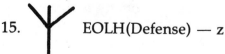

15.   EOLH (Defense) — z

Another rune that appears to be connected with an older symbol—the splayed human hand which it resembles, an instinctive sign for warding off harm. Outlines of the human hand have been discovered in caves where prehistoric men once lived. The American Indians used this sign for peace. Similar symbols, but with five branches, are used in North Africa to turn aside the evil eye.

A reasonable objection can be made that if Eolh is meant to represent the human hand, it should have five branches. In fact, it is one of the less understood runes. In later rune poems it seems to have stood for elk-sedge, which may be a tough kind of marsh grass that elk fed upon. But it has also been interpreted as willow, sea-holly, swan, and even as the sign of an obscure god named Alcis mentioned by Tacitus.

One thing at least is known: the rune was carried by warriors to protect them in battle. In the *Old English Rune Poem* the connotation of warding off survives:

> Elk-sedge usually dwells in a marsh,
> growing in the water; it gives grievous wounds
> staining with blood every man
> who lays a hand on it.

Anyone who as a child has tried to tear up a handful of marsh ferns will understand all too well what is meant here. The fibers in the stems of the ferns part and cut like razors through the skin. This verse is very similar to the one representing Thorn.

In the *Norwegian Rune Poem*, Eolh is linked with the claw of a hawk. Pictorially, this is the best correspondence. In the burial mound of a shaman discovered near Copenhagen the claw of a falcon was found along with other magical articles. The talons of a hawk are the focus of its power; with them it catches and kills its prey. The Teutonic peoples would have a knowledge of their great strength. Very likely the mummified claws of hawks were used magically to embody the speed, nobility and power of these great birds. Among the American Indians the eagle occupied a prominent place in the magical hierarchy.

Whatever the rune may have originally stood for, its abstracted meaning is generally agreed upon—stay away or suffer unpleasant consequences. It is a kind of shield which the person who presents it erects before him.

Magically, it is used for defense on all levels: physical, emotional and intellectual. It protects against the attacks of men, beasts or spirits. It can be sent to another to keep him safe from harm. Eolh figures prominently in the protective charm worn during dangerous rune rituals which will be described in a later chapter.

16. ⟨ Also ᛋ SIGEL (Sun) — s

Sigel stands for the rays that emanate from the sun and strike the earth—its active power. The shape suggests a bolt of lightning, and in the Tarot card of The Tower, lightning is shown lashing from the solar orb to destroy a stone tower, which is usually associated with the Tower of Babel.

The Nazis recognized the destructive potential of this rune when they chose it as the insignia of the SS. Indeed, the Swastika is no more than two Sigel runes laid over each other to suggest the whirling, flaming ball of a falling meteor. In pagan times, meteors were looked upon as weapons of the gods, particularly Thor whose hammer was earlier thought to be a meteorite.

The Germans worshipped the sun. Caesar mentions sun worship, and the numerous sun wheels found in the rock carvings attest to it, as do certain relics such as the bronze altar found near Ystad in Sweden. This last is a remarkable object shaped roughly like a drum. It stands on ten bronze wheels arrayed around its perimeter, and its top is inscribed with concentric circles and rings of fire that form a solar image of impressive proportions.

The offensive power suggested by the shape of the Sigel rune is well represented by this verse from the *Icelandic Rune Poem*:

> Sun is shield of the sky
> and shining ray
> and destroyer of ice.

Magically, Sigel is a sword of justice, the retribution of the gods. It is used to destroy enemies and to strike through confusion to the heart of problems. Sigel is an offensive weapon just as Eolh is a defensive weapon. It is used to punish; its effects are similar to the sword of ritual magic. Since it is an instrument of Light, it cannot be used to commit evil with impunity. Attempts to pervert it to the uses of darkness end tragically.

17. ↑ TYR (Tiw) — t

Tyr begins and names the third *aett* of the German *futhark*. One of the major Teutonic gods of prehistoric times, by the period when Roman historians began to record German customs, he had degenerated into a minor war deity and was ignobly compared to Mars. However, from what can be gathered of his nature, he deserved better. His great courage was restrained by his intelligence and sense of honor. The blind killing rage characteristic of Mars was not part of Tiw's original makeup. He was the god of legal and moral judgment, the upholder of oaths. He could be more closely compared to Mercury than Mars, since both Tiw and Mercury were instruments of a higher law.

Leaving his early nature aside, the latter day Tiw was a war god. The rune (↑) is similar to the symbol for Mars (♂). It was cut into weapons and carried into battle to give courage and war skill. It occurs on many rune charms. The similarity in shape of Tyr to all piercing weapons, particularly the spear, is significant. The favorite weapon of the Germans was a short light spear called a *framea*, which they had the option of casting at a foe or retaining for close combat.

In the *Old English Rune Poem*, the meaning of Tyr has developed into a constellation or star or planet in the night sky. Even then it retains its connotations of faithfulness and dependability:

> Tyr is one of the guiding signs, it keeps faith well
> with princes; always it holds its course
> above the night clouds; it never fails.

This late definition may refer to the planet Mars or to a constellation of stars. Perhaps it is the North Star, which is symbolized on maps and charts with the sign: ⅄ . The North Star is certainly a guide, always holds its course, and never fails.

Magically, Tyr is similar to Sigel in that both are offensive weapons, but Tyr refrs more specifically to human qualities of courage and determination. It lends its strength in battles of all kinds, supports failing limbs and guides weapons to their mark. When carved on a weapon, it helps it to strike true and keeps it from shattering. Cast on another person with evil intent, it carries strife on all levels. Can cause fist fights or wrestlings with conscience depending on how it is modified by circumstance and the runes that accompany it.

18. ᛒ BEORC (Birch) — b

The birch figures prominently in Teutonic customs as the symbol of spring awakening. It is the first tree in the northern forests to turn green after the long winter. In the *Golden Bough* Frazer describes how the Russian villagers would cut down a young birch tree in the spring, dress it in a woman's clothes and honor it with feasts and celebrations, then throw it into a stream. Frazer believed this last act to be a rain charm, but it was more likely a fertility charm. A variation of this custom was to dress the prettiest girl in the village completely in birch boughs.

The slender trunk of the birch, its delicate leaves and silver bark which has the appearance of adornment, all contribute to ascribing feminine qualities to it. Likely it was related to Freyja, the goddess noted for her love of ornament and the most beautiful female in Asgard.

Birch twigs were placed in houses and stables to cause women and mares to conceive. Both men and women were lashed with birch twigs for a similar purpose. In modern Scandinavia, the custom endures in connection with the sauna. Until recent times school children all over Europe were beaten with birch to make their minds fertile. In Cheshire it used to be the practice to fix a sprig of birch over the door of a lover. Birch bark prevents scurvy and has other healing virtues. The smoke of the burning wood is aromatic and pleasant.

Generally, the rune signifies health, beauty and love. It encourages fertility and growth and renews the life force. It causes women to bear children. The effect of Beorc is opposite that of its pair rune, Tyr, which brings destruction.

Magically, Beorc can be used to heal and comfort in times of hardship. It may be cast as a love charm, or used maliciously to arouse uncontrolled passions. However, it can only be perverted with difficulty since its nature encourages a healthful balance. Esoterically it serves as a doorway to the understanding of the life-giving powers of the earth.

19.   ᛖ   EH (Horse) — e

The horse was more than just a means of transportation to the early Germans. It was a sacred animal related to the cult of the sun. The sun was envisioned as riding across the heavens in his chariot drawn by shining steeds. Tacitus writes in his *Germania*:

> Kept at public expense in these same (consecrated) woods and groves are white horses, pure from the taint of earthly labor; these are yoked to a sacred car, and accompanied by the priest and the king, or chief of the tribe, who note their neighings and snortings.

At Trundholm, Denmark was discovered a bronze chariot which represents the solar disk being drawn by a horse. The disk was originally covered in gold leaf, most of which has fallen off. Both horse and chariot are mounted on wheels, perhaps to be pulled along in a procession. The wheels are of four spokes and very similar to the ten wheels that support the solar altar described under the Sigel rune. This model of the chariot of the sun has been dated by some authorities as early as 1000 B.C.

Chariot of the Sun. **Bronze and gold leaf. 1000 B.C.**
Believed to have been used for ritual purposes. It suggest the importance of
both the Sun and the horse in early Teutonic worship.

—Reproduced by permission of the Danish National Museum

The snortings of the sacred white horses were used as auguries by the priests, who looked upon the horses as messengers of the gods. It is worth mentioning in passing the beautiful White Horse of Berkshire, England—a gigantic stylized horse carved in the crest of a hill which can only be properly seen from the air. The horse was probably a sacred animal for all Europe as far back as the Stone Age.

On the material plane the horse symbolized grace, speed and strength—the physical virtues. Beauty of form and function. It was not an end in itself but the means to an end. A medium through which the desires of men might be accomplished.

Magically, this rune can be used as the means to solve a problem. Cast, it can render a person a beast of burden to be used for a given end. It generates the vehicle for accomplishing the will. Mundanely, it provides transportation. Esoterically, it carries the spirit forward over obstacles.

20. ᛗ MAN (Man) — m

Paired with Eh is the Man rune, which can be translated as human being, or perhaps as Mannus, the Germanic Adam and the archetypical pattern of the race. In the rune poems it is used simply as everyman, the consensus of opinion being: "man is the augmentation of the dust." This rather depressing note is maintained through all the major rune poems. The notion of man is linked with the inevitability of death. Man equals mortal.

Certainly the Teutons saw enough of their kin slaughtered to have no illusions about human grandeur. One of the rune stones reads: "Vidken the priest wrote me, and here I shall stand for a while"—showing that not even the stones were looked upon as permanent. The pessimistic tone of the rune poems may be due to the influence of Christianity and should not be projected back onto the pagan roots of the runes.

Qualities that distinguish humanity from the beasts are intelligence, speech and free will. The rune Man stands for the mental virtues. Other facets of Man are the power of imagination, the urge to worship and the manipulation of the environment. It is the human soul that energizes these abilities.

Magically, Man is used to evoke the powers of the intellect. Ulysses escaping the Cyclops radiated Man. It calls forth the cunning and daring of the Trickster. This rune is the sign of the cunning man and the wise woman. It provides the method to an end.

21.   LAGU (Water) — l

The form of Lagu suggests a broken reed. It means water, particularly the sea but also rivers, fountains and falls. Water is a complex symbol with both positive and negative connotations. It stands for fertility in the form of rain and streams, but also for the underworld of nightmarish monsters when presented as a dark still lake, or for the capricious destroyer of ships as the roiling ocean. As a general rule standing pools and brackish water is harmful, while clear, moving water is beneficial.

Travel by ship was easier in ancient times than land travel. Most people who had not spent their entire lives in one place were familiar with the power of the waves, the initial terror of going out of sight of land, and the sense of utter dependence upon the caprice of fate.

Water was the black realm of the unknown that men crossed fearfully, having no idea what lay below the surface. It was equivalent to the depths of the unconscious which the awareness cannot plumb. It represented the obsessive and perverse side of sexuality when unalloyed with the solar light. In Teutonic mythology, the undines (water spirits) are beautiful maidens who pull men under the surface to their deaths. Their songs induce madness. Yet water cannot be shunned, not even its frightful aspects, since it is a necessity of daily life.

Magically, Lagu is a rune of mystery that can be connected with the powers of the moon. Causes dreams and visions. Madness. False pregnancies. Suicides. Irrational and unnatural crimes.

It can be used to look into the future but is not to be trusted. Changeable. However, when all dreams and hopes have dried up, a small measure of Lagu can be an initiator of change and growth. The symbol of the Cup as it is understood in modern magic represents the more wholesome qualities of Lagu.

22. ◇ Also ⬜ and ✕ ING (Fertility god) — ng

Ing was a god of the Danes. The Old English word *Ingwine* means friends of Ing, and is applied to the Danes in *Beowolf*. Tacitus mentions a tribe living near the Baltic Sea called the *Ingaevanes*. The *Old English Rune Poem* reads:

> Ing among the East-Danes was first
> beheld by men, until that later time when to the east
> he made his departure over the waves, followed by
>   his chariot;
> that was the name those stern warriors gave the hero.

The god Frey, who was the Teutonic male fertility deity, is said to have had another name, *Yngvi*. His descendants were called *Ynglingar*. Since Frey was the son of Nerthus, the earth mother, and traveled in a chariot, Ing is supposed to have been a fertility god, but this is only supposition. The *Old English Rune Poem* describes him as a hero.

It is interesting that his departure across the seas to the east is said to be in front of his chariot. One would assume that he would ride inside it. Perhaps he was the invisible traveler in a physical model of the sacred car, like Nerthus. Something may have caused him to remove himself across the sea—the coming of Christianity?—and his sacred chariot may have been shipped after him.

When Ing is viewed paired with Lagu, it should be noted that the god crosses the water. The crossing of water was a common euphemism for the passage into the underworld. Ing is a god who has gone away, like the great heroes whose bodies were pushed into the sea after their departed souls on burning warships. The chariot of Ing which follows after him is the lifeless, hollow vessel of the god.

Ing may have been a god of the hearth, a protector of the family and house, an insurer of good catches of fish and good crops. He would represent the healthy and productive side of sexuality. Lagu is the power and influence of waters—Ing the power and influence of the earth.

Magically, the rune can be used to overcome illusions and mental illness. It serves as a help in practical day-to-day problems but should not be underrated on that account. Ing is a powerful force for good. It protects the home and those within it. Calms domestic strife. Unites families with bonds of affection. A down-to-earth deity embodying the simple but precious human virtues that lie close to the land.

23. ⟩⟨ Also ᛗ DAEG (Day) — d

Usually Daeg is interpreted as the light of day and linked with the sun cult. The *Old English Rune Poem* calls Daeg the "glorious light of the Creator, a source of joy and hope." In the light of day, the horrors of darkness are impotent. The light of day is an earthly manifestation of the more ethereal Light of the divine Spirit. If Ken is the artificial light of the torch in the halls of men, Daeg is the natural light of the sky. Ken is the Spirit acting through man in the form of the human virtues; Daeg is the Spirit acting through Nature to create the beauties of the greater world.

Daeg may also be interpreted as a period of time in which the light strengthens, reaches its maximum power, and then declines. For the Germans the day began in darkness. Tacitus, the Roman historian who recorded the fact, found it very strange:

> Instead of reckoning the days as we do, they reckon by nights, and in this manner fix both their ordinary and their legal appointments. Night they regard as bringing on the day.

The passage of the sun across the sky may be likened to the

passage of a human soul through its earthly life. It begins in the darkness of the womb; birth is like the dawn; the fullness of manhood comes at noon; old age brings a dimness to the sight, a kind of twilight; and death seals the eyelids on darkness once again.

In the abstract, Daeg can signify completeness or totality. The span of a process or thing. A circle that defines limits. A name—in the sense that the sum of a life is its name before God. The period of existence. It should be distinguished from Ger which stands for a revolution or inversion.

Magically, the rune can be used to complete anything that is ongoing or unfinished. Used maliciously it can cause death. It concludes battles and love affairs. It encourages completion according to the natural laws of the gods. Can also be used to define limits and set amounts. In its other sense, as the light of Nature, Daeg can be used to banish the oppressing influence of a hostile environment.

24. 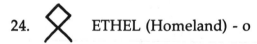 ETHEL (Homeland) - o

In early usage, this rune indicated the land of birth in the narrow sense of the immediate locality where the tribe or clan dwelt. Land was important to the Germans. Families preferred to live some distance from one another rather than clustered together in villages and towns. They cleared a wide swarth around the house, probably as a defense against surprise attacks. The origin of Ethel may have been this circular clearing.

As Teutonic societies evolved, the sense of the rune was modified first to mean inherited land, and then inherited property. Used in this broad way, Ethel stood for the sum of earthly possessions accumulated by a man in his lifetime—what came down to him from his forefathers, the gifts of chiefs, the spoils of war and the craft of his own hands.

Landed property is the generally accepted meaning of the Ethel rune, which stands last in the traditional *futhark*. It complements Feoh, the first rune of the alphabet, one of whose meanings is moveable possessions. The two types of possessions were inter-dependent in that cattle, the most important moveable possession of the early Germans, needed land to graze on, and land without cattle was of little value.

Enlarging the meaning of the rune yields native country or nation of birth. This is a natural evolution of the rune, just as any nation grows up from the amalgamated holdings of family clans. The use of Ethel to stand for the soul of a nation would not be unreasonable in modern magical practice.

If Daeg represents the span of a human life, Ethel may be said to stand for the accomplishments of that life on earth. Every man's native land is that which he carves out and holds on to; morally as well as materially. Good and evil actions are passed down to the next generation as its inescapable inheritance. The human laws of legal inheritance are only imitations of this natural law.

Magically, Ethel can be made to embody property or possessions. Cast with favor it brings increase; cast with malice it carries loss. Care must be taken in sending it so that the inheritance, whatever type it is, does not come as the result of the death of a loved one. The runes are pitiless and interpret instructions literally.

These are the 24 characters of the German *futhark*. There is some argument over the order of the final pair of runes. In the *Old English Rune Poem*, Ethel comes before Daeg. However, the way the runes are ordered above is generally accepted as the earliest sequence, and the later inversion of Ethel and Daeg as an aberration.

When the runes traveled to England with the Anglo-Saxons, they were increased to 28 characters. The four new runes are listed below:

25.   AC (Oak) — a

A common tree in the English forest. Important for its acorns which provided food for livestock, and its wood which was used to build ships and other structures where mass and strength were required. Frazer calls the oak "pre-eminently the sacred tree of the Aryans" and links it to the fire festivals. The sacred fire, he says, was kindled by friction of oak wood, and the original Yule logs were of oak. Oak fed the fires of Vesta and the perpetual flame of Romove, a Lithuanian sanctuary.

Frazer also links the oak to the myth of Balder and the mistletoe. Mistletoe is a parasitic plant that grows on oaks. Since it is evergreen, it would appear as the constant renewal of life when seen in the dead of winter against the leafless boughs of its host. From the oak, the body of Balder slain and burned, springs the mistletoe, the renewed spirit of the god.

26. ᚫ AESC (Ash) — ae

Not to be confused with the Os rune, which in the Anglo-Saxon *futhorc* takes the form ᚩ. The similarity may have arisen from the fact that Os stands for Odin, and the ash tree is sacred to Odin.

The most famous ash is Yggdrasill, the world tree. Ash was used for making weapons, particularly the shafts of spears. The spear was the primary weapon of the Germanic tribes and may have had magical associations for the Anglo-Saxons.

The *Old English Rune Poem* gives the character of ash wood:

> The ash is extremely tall, precious to mankind,
> strong on its base; it holds the ground as it should,
> although many men attack it.

The verse may refer to the resistance of the tree to felling or to its military function. It may even be a reference to Yggdrasill, which holds the fabric of the world together though foolish and base men seek to overthrow the natural order.

27. ᛦ Also ᛦ YR (Saddle) — y

Usually translated as bow, but this is unsatisfactory. A better meaning seems to be saddle in the context of the *Old English Rune Poem*:

> A saddle (?) is a pleasure and brings honor
> to all princes and nobles; it looks fine on a steed,
> is reliable on a journey, a kind of army-gear.

Saddle is a contraction for yew-wood-saddle-bow. Elaborate saddles probably were not common when this poem was written, perhaps as early as the eighth century. Bow can be made to fit the verse, as can horn—a conjectured alternative. Other less likely speculations are adornment, axe-iron and gold-buckle.

28.   EAR (Earth) — ea

The general meaning of Ear, the final rune in the first extension of the Anglo-Saxon *futhorc*, is earth, but it is used in such a narrow sense in the *Old English Rune Poem* that it has also been translated as grave and house of the dead, and even as the end:

> Earth is loathsome to every man,
> when irresistibly the flesh,
> the dead body begins to grow cold,
> the livid one to choose earth as its bedfellow;
> fruits fail, joys vanish, man-made covenants are broken.

The type of earth intended is not only the earth of the grave but the moldering flesh of the corpse. It is in this sense that man is described as the "augmentation of the dust."

In its second extension, five new runes were added to the Anglo-Saxon *futhorc*, bringing the total number to 33. This was a late local addition that probably took place in the ninth century and was confined to Northumbria. There is little that can be said about this last set of runes. They have no long tradition of use or profound magical meaning. They were included in the rune alphabet to serve the technical requirements of language and in this sense are artificial.

29. ᚼ IOR (Amphibian) — io

This rune has been translated variously as eel, newt, snake and even sea. None of these meanings are entirely satisfactory. This is the only rune of the five later additions to occur in the *Old English Rune Poem*, but its context is so ambiguous that a certain meaning cannot be derived:

> The amphibian (?) belongs to the river fish;
>   yet it always takes
> its food on land; it has a beautiful dwelling place,
> surrounded by water, where it lives in delight.

Perhaps a water plant or tree of some kind, or a type of frog, or even a water fowl.

30. ᛣ CALC (Cup) — k

May mean chalice, or beaker. Other less useful translations are sandal, shoe, and chalk. There is almost nothing to go on in trying to derive a meaning for this rune. However, for magical purposes, cup is the most powerful and evocative of the options.

31. ᚸ GAR (Spear) — g

Here the sense is more definite. The spear has already been discussed as a German arm. The great spear of Teutonic legend was Gungnir, the spear of Odin which nothing could turn from its mark. It had been fashioned by dwarfs and was emblematic of the keen perception and unrelenting will of its owner.

32. CWEORD (Unknown) — q

Because the meaning of this rune is unknown, some scholars have suggested that it is meaningless; merely a sound, like the letters of modern English. This seems unlikely since all other runes have intelligible names. However, no meaning for Cweord has been put forward.

33. STAN (Stone) — st

Stone was regarded in prehistoric times as a living substance, the dwelling place of spirits. There are mountains in Silesia once thought to be petrified bodies of giants. Dwarfs dwelt in stone caverns and were jealous of the treasures of the earth. Thor's hammer, Mjolnir, was in early times thought to be made of stone.

When altars were raised, a natural stone was used, unhewn by chisel and hammer. The monuments of the early peoples of Europe are also of unhewn stone. In historic times, stones became important as monuments on which runes were inscribed with a recording function.

Chapter 5

RITUAL METHOD

Magic rituals have certain basic elements in common. For the sake of mnemonics, these may be called the six "p's:"

1. Purpose
2. Preparation
3. Purification
4. Protection
5. Performance
6. Peroration

Purpose

No ritual is possible without a purpose since all stages in a ritual tend toward a definite goal. Without a purpose, a ritual would be meaningless play acting. This is precisely what many modern rituals have become: the ritual of marriage, for example, where two people pledge themselves to each other for the rest of their lives. For many couples this is an act of premeditated hypocrisy.

In primitive cultures, unconscious desire in the members

of the group gives rise to physical actions which over the course of time become formalized, and still later receive simplistic rationalizations. The rites of primitive man are never deliberately invented. Although they have their individual proponents, they grow from deeply rooted social needs. It is also desire that shapes the rituals of modern magic. However, modern rituals spring from individual needs, and are at least in part consciously formed.

The advantage the modern Magus has over the primitive shaman is that the former knows the process that occurs between desire and ritual, and seeks to facilitate the discovery of the perfect ritual form to suit his specific need. He is aware of the vast spectrum of ritual patterns that have been used in the past and can extract from them certain general elements upon which to build his personal rite.

When something is gained, something else is lost. The Magus tends to be out of touch with his instincts. He is less able to judge which ritual will be effective and which will be mere empty words and gestures. He relies too much on authority, not enough on his inner guiding sense of rightness. The grimoires of magic, originally the subjective experiments of individuals, become for the Magus inflexible molds into which he vainly tries to force his unique requirements.

This is the value of a clearly expressed purpose. It provides a guide for the selection of the appropriate ritual pattern. The primitive shaman has no need to express his desire—it forms the ritual directly in the forge of his subconscious. In intellectualizing magic and bringing it into the conscious realm, the Magus must reason and express his desire if it is to act as the ritual pattern-maker; otherwise the ritual will be purposeless and impotent.

When the Magus holds his purpose clearly in mind, a reaction will occur deep in his subconscious and ritual forms will arise for his consideration. He then must compare the purpose to the form and determine with the aid of reason if the two are compatible. Reason alone can never create a ritual, but it can scrutinize it to determine its viability.

Nothing clarifies an idea better than an attempt to communicate it. For this reason it is customary to write out at length all rituals before attempting to conduct them. This precept should also be applied to the ritual purpose. Oftentimes the Magus will not fully comprehend what he wants until he sees it before him on the page. Writing out the purpose clarifies it not only consciously, but on the deeper levels of his mind.

All purposes in ritual magic must be lawful. They must harmonize with the positive evolutionary progress of the universe. These evolutionary laws have been given to men in human terms through the revelations of the prophets. The Ten Commandments revealed to Moses on Mount Sinai are an example. The truth of a revealed law can be determined by comparing it with other precepts granted by God to humanity through the ages. True laws are life affirming. They support love, hope, faith, happiness and all the human virtues.

If a ritual purpose is in discordance with divine law, the ritual based on it will bring only disaster upon the head of the person who attempts to work it. The angels will turn their faces away and leave the Magus to the malicious manipulations of demons. These may give the ritual the appearance of success to tempt the Magus into a deeper involvement with them, but ultimately, all magic in opposition to the laws of heaven is destructive.

Preparation

Preparations for ritual stem naturally from a clearly understood purpose and are impossible without it. They include such things as: 1) the management of time so that the Magus will be available when the ritual may best be conducted; 2) the securing and making ready of the ritual place, which will be private and free from intrusion; 3) the manufacture of instruments and preparation of materials; 4) any physical or mental groundwork that must be laid such as particular study and memorization, rehearsal of difficult movements, and strengthening exercises; 5) the actual formulation of the ritual and its writing down and rehearsal until it becomes second nature.

1. Major rituals require a great deal of time; indeed, an astonishing length of time to the uninitiated. Rituals covering months are not unknown. The serious Magus must realize the span of his ritual and make a commitment to provide the necessary time for its conscientious fulfillment or the ritual cannot succeed. Perfunctory rituals are a mockery of the higher powers they seek to evoke. They will result in frustration and perhaps have destructive consequences.

Not all rituals are lengthy. Some can be done in a matter of hours or even minutes by an accomplished adept who has a space set aside and instruments and materials ready, who fully understands his Art, is in a state of purity, and is accustomed to composing ritual forms. However, any ritual by its nature sets its own timetable. It cannot be rushed. A close attention to his inner sense of propriety will tell the Magus when to act and when to wait.

2. Rune Magic is closely bound to Nature. If possible it should be done out of doors in early morning or evening when the air is still, unless the ritual dictates a particular time and place. Outdoor rituals will only be possible for those who live deep in the country or have access to a private walled garden, since magical workings must never be observed by outsiders.

A room can be used, but it should have symbolic associations of Nature in it and should be exposed to fresh air and sunlight. An airless, windowless basement is about the worst possible setting for rune magic. Ritual chambers can often be adapted to suit rune magic by hanging in fresh boughs, strewing the floor with pine or spruce needles, placing a flat, unhewn stone on top of the altar, lighting the chamber in green and gold, or playing one of the readily available tapes or records of Nature sounds.

3. The general instruments of ceremonial magic can often be used in rune magic, although they are not strictly necessary. Also, the common materials of ceremonial magic can at times be employed. Essential are instruments for making the runes: knife, pen, scribe, stains and pigments; and materials to make the runes upon: paper, wood, wax and metal disks. The ritual purpose will dictate any special needs. Only those instruments and materials directly involved in the ritual should be present during its enactment.

4. Physical and mental preparations of a purely utilitarian kind may be required. For example, a ritual in which the Magus must hold a difficult sitting position for a long time may need practicing before it can be endured. It may be necessary to master a particular rhythm of breathing, or an intricate gesture. A ritual may demand some symbolic or mythological association of which the Magus has less than perfect knowledge.

5. Above all the ritual must be understood and thoroughly memorized before it is attempted. It is not enough to write it down and keep the paper in hand while stumbling through the steps. It must be known in the heart as well as the head. It has been said that actors make the best ritualists. This is true only when they practice the Stanislavski method and identify themselves wholly with their roles. A ritual is a type of dramatic presentation with the gods for an audience. Its message can only be effectively conveyed if the actor has utter faith and belief in it. He must understand that it is true. He must feel the power of it.

Purification

Genuine magic is impossible without purity. It is purity of purpose, of will, of desire that gives a magical process its power. Purity taps the life force of the human center, which is the Higher Self and the doorway to the Unmanifest. Only the One has the strength to create the many.

Man cannot command the gods of pagan mythology unless he gains authority from the transcendent All-Father. Otherwise the lesser gods will become demons who will make the Magus their dupe. While he believes himself to be commanding them they will be manipulating him, drawing him ever farther from the Light, his sole source of strength and protection, and biding their time until he is weak and confused enough to become their unquestioning tool.

The ways of purity are many, since every religion and sect acknowledges its prime importance and has developed methods for its attainment. All forms of asceticism are exercises in purifying the will. Purity is misunderstood in the West. It is thought to be a kind of weakness. In fact, it is a type of strength. Whenever the will overrules the wish, purity is increased. True will is always in harmony with the will of God.

Adepts who practice degraded sex magic, sacrifice of animals, torture, self-mutilation and so on to increase their will are deluding themselves in a pitiful manner. They embrace the arguments of the lower demons who only desire to use and destroy them, because they instinctively recognize that, although it seems hard, the path of darkness is the easy way, while the path of Light which seems easy is the hard way.

Any child can pretend to itself that it is a great and powerful being while it is leading a bear on a leash, until the bear chooses to go in a different direction. The exponents of black magic are in the position of the child. They trade immediate self-aggrandizement for true and lasting power. The dark forces are happy to pay what to them is a trifling cost for the permanent enslavement of misguided adepts. This is the drama of Faust enacted on the stage of life.

The elements of purity are self-denial and hardship which strengthens the will, stillness and peace which allows the inner voice to speak, and prayer which shapes the soul to the laws of God. Outer purity—washing, anointing with oil, careful regard to dress and appearance—is only useful when it is a symbolic reflection of an inner evolution. Thus a bath may be used to represent the cleansing of the soul.

For the untrained person to purify himself for a major ritual requires at least a month. He should eat lightly and only when necessary, but not starve himself. Dress in plain clothing kept scrupulously clean. Sleep as little as he requires and always rise with the sun. Bathe and wash often with a clear awareness of the significance of the act. Avoid frivolous talk and company, entertainments, and all excesses and habits such as drinking, smoking, hard exercise, and all sexual associations. Contemplate his ritual desire and pray for worthiness.

This is a harsh road; impossibly harsh for those not suited to it. Many are attracted by the gleam and ornament of magic. Few are willing to endure, or even undertake, the tempering of their beings required to make the grand illusion a reality. Perhaps they recognize that the process of purification is one that will change them and they fear that change. Yet no normal, average man or woman is capable of a magical act. To be a Magus is to be apart—not necessarily better, certainly not happier, but different from common humanity.

Protection

There are forces in heaven and earth undreamed of in most philosophies. What is more, many of them delight in the perversion and destruction of the human soul. No ritual should be considered without also planning in advance the steps necessary for protection.

The dangers of magic are psychical. Only by reaction do they become physical. Entities attack through the mind. The mind is the access spirits have into the human world. They play upon the emotions by manipulating desires and fears. They test the intellect by challenging accepted moral foundations. They distract the senses and cause illusions both attractive and horrifying for the same purpose of luring the Magus off his spiritual path.

The danger becomes physical when such entities succeed in unbalancing the mind of their victim, and self-destructive or murderous impulses arise that his weakened will can no longer cope with. Accidents, suicides, inexplicable aggressions, etc. can often be attributed to the manipulations of evil spirits. Many senseless crimes have possession as a root cause.

There is another lesser-known danger. When evil spirits discover they cannot command the mind of their intended victim directly, they seek to harm him indirectly by entering the bodies of other men or animals close to him. Those with psychic vision can see such demons peering out through the eyes of men, women and even children who are totally unaware that they are the host of a supernatural intelligence. Friends will suddenly become foes. Arguments and fights will erupt for no reason. The victim will feel the social atmosphere around him pervaded with hostility.

Magical protections are of three kinds: 1) Barriers; 2) Counter-forces; 3) Appeals to divine mercy.

1. The best known barrier is the magic circle. It is often physically inscribed on the ground or floor of the ritual place, but is invariably formed in the astral world of the imagination. Drawn around the Magus at the beginning of a ritual from the inside in a sunwise direction, to the degree that it is accepted as real by its maker it will have power. Trained adepts have the ability to visualize the circle so intensely that it becomes tangible.

An analogous barrier is the aura, an imaginary egg-shaped envelope said to surround the human body. The aura is not material but purely mental, and for this reason cannot be measured by machines. The weak electromagnetic charge that emanates from the surface of the skin is often mistaken for the aura by materialists, but the two have little in common. Many adepts strengthen or harden the edges of their auras to prevent the ingress of malevolent forces. This is done by compressing the aura in the imagination until it glows more intensely and forms a kind of loose second skin.

A third useful barrier is the cross. Even without the many Christian overtones it now carries, the cross is a symbol of considerable power. It has the effect of stilling change and balancing opposing forces, and acts as a symbolic preservative. Drawn over the body it is a magical shield against attack. The cross mainly used in magic is the Celtic, with equal arms and a circle surrounding the point of intersection: ⊕ . However the Christian cross is also effective.

At the root of all three protective devices is the general notion that the Magus can divide himself off from the rest of the world. All people at the time of their birth erect their own personal magical barrier at the limit of their body. The body, and the mind which they perceive as inside the body, they regard as wholly their domain. Whatever the human mind believes becomes real. It is this rock solid conviction in the mind of modern man that his body is inviolable which keeps hostile psychic entities from manipulating him.

Once a person begins to doubt that inviolability, as must happen during the study of magic, the barrier begins to crumble, and other beings gain access to the human awareness. In their milder forms they reveal themselves as audible and visible hallucinations, obsessing thoughts, tactile sensations, and occur most frequently on the border of sleep and wakefulness when the guards of the mind are lowered.

To remain sane and strong, the Magus must devise methods of protection that support his weakened sense of the limits of his own house of flesh, which to magical eyes has walls of glass. These are especially needed during actual rituals when psychic entities are invited to approach. The circle, the hardened aura, the cross—all act as passive barriers that strengthen the blurred margin between inside and outside.

2. A more direct form of magical protection is the countering of force with force. This defense relies on the principle that opposing energies will neutralize each other. If attacked by psychic Fire, for example, one recourse is to evoke elemental Water. The two touching become Air. If afflicted by a darkness of the soul, spiritual Light can be used to dispel it. Since Light is a positive force, one spark is sufficient to banish negative darkness.

These and other potencies are projected through the medium of symbols. The pentagram controls elemental forces and can be used to call them forth or send them away depending on how it is drawn. The powers of the elements are the most useful magical potencies for an active defense.

To invoke or call up an elemental force, draw the pentagram of that element clockwise in the air with a continuous line starting and ending at the point of the pentagram assigned to the element. To banish or send away an elemental force draw the figure in reverse, beginning and ending at the point of the pentagram of the element you wish to banish and proceeding in a counterclockwise direction. If the attacker can be perceived, draw the pentagram between yourself and the threat. If the attack has no perceptible direction, draw the pentagram toward the direction of the element, given below:

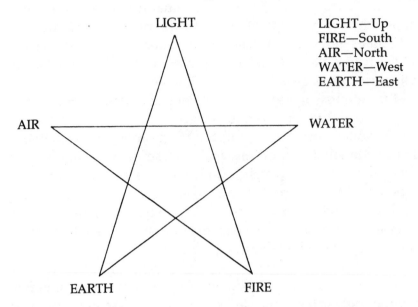

LIGHT—Up
FIRE—South
AIR—North
WATER—West
EARTH—East

Sometimes it will be best to simply disperse the oppressing force with the appropriate banishing pentagram. At other times it may be better to counter one element by invoking its opposite. This is a matter of individual discretion and the circumstances of the moment.

It should be pointed out that other magical texts give a different procedure for drawing the pentagram, and different assignments of the elements to the points of the compass. The method presented here is simpler and more rational than that used in most magical practice, but both are equally effective for those who understand and believe in them.*

---

* The system developed by the Hermetic Order of the Golden Dawn in the last century is virtually universal. In it elements are invoked by drawing the first line segment of the pentagram toward the element, and banished by drawing the first line segment away, except in the case of Light where *two* pentagrams of a different construction are drawn to invoke, and *two* to banish.

For the traditional way of drawing the pentagram, and assigning the elements to the quarters, see *The Golden Dawn*, Llewellyn Publications, Book IV, "The Ritual of the Pentagram." For a complete examination of the new system presented here versus the traditional system, see *The New Magus*, Llewellyn Publications, Part I, "Pentagram."

3. When all defense fails, a last resort is to call upon the mercy and protection of God. This guard is all powerful when spoken with a sincere and contrite heart; worthless if used hypocritically. As it is all too often a last desperate resort, even the most cynical, in the extremity of their terror, can often manage a sincere moment. For this reason a prayer for divine mercy may save those who are considered beyond redemption.

Performance

The body of a ritual is always unique because it is formed directly on the object of desire. It is a dramatic presentation of the wish fulfilled using symbols as actors and the magic circle as a stage. The Magus is the writer-producer-director. The audience consists of the gods or spirits at whom the ritual is aimed. They are invited to participate actively in the drama.

Good rituals exercise all the senses. The senses of the Magus are the windows through which spirits observe the ritual. This is true whether they are invoked or evoked; that is, whether they appear inside the self or outside the circle. Through the eyes of the Magus, spirits see their symbolic colors and designs. Through his nose they smell the scents most pleasing to them. Through his ears they hear the sounds that invite them to attend the drama. To better actualize the ritual the Magus dances or gestures in pre-set patterns, speaks his desires in a sonorous voice, and tries to experience to the utmost all the elements he has gathered together.

One symbol or set of symbols represents the object of desire, which may be a person, place, or thing that he wants to change in a specific way. Other symbols represent the forces he wishes to act on that object. The way these symbols are brought together is the desire finding fulfillment.

To take a brief example, consider the so-called voodoo dolls used in primitive and not so primitive societies to inflict pain or death on other human beings. The doll is the focus of the magical will. The pins represent the kind of suffering it is desired to inflict. The piercing of the body of the doll with the pins is a dramatic enactment of the desire realized.

During a ritual the Magus experiences an inner state of intense concentration. This is never strained. On the contrary, it must be effortless. He becomes the drama he is enacting to such an extent that he forgets the self-consciousness that divides him from the center of all being. At the same time he retains some awareness of self in order to hold his purpose, which is ego motivated. A duality of mind is necessary in which the conscious identity of the Magus is pushed to the background, but still remains in control.

At the climax of a ritual the Magus will feel a moment of release in which his pent-up desire suddenly escapes into the depths of his subconscious. This sensation is difficult to describe to those who have never experienced it, but it is equivalent to the popping open of a steam valve that allows excess internal pressure to vent out. It is not sexual and should not be confused with sexual release. This is a common error.

Peroration

After the conclusion of the drama, a final prayer is made which recapitulates the purpose of the ritual and invites the favor of the gods. This serves to clarify and emphasize the meaning of what has just taken place. The final prayer must be composed to suit the ritual and is therefore always unique.

The ritual is concluded by reversing the steps that opened it. Psychic forces are banished from the region of the circle with signs and names of power. The circle is drawn back into the point of the Higher Self by retracing it widdershins. The Magus then recrosses his body to preserve himself from unforeseen harm and carefully puts away the ritual instruments and materials in the reverse order to which they were taken out. All magical objects are treated with utmost reverence.

When the ritual has been concluded, concern about realizing the magical desire must be submerged into the subconscious, and outwardly the Magus must become tranquil. Calm is necessary because what is present at that critical time in the awareness may cause ripples in the subconscious. The conscious willing of an event actually prevents its realization.

Athletes know this phenomenon all too well. A goal intensely hoped for is never realized, but once hope is relaxed it is attained with ease.

The magical desire will be realized seemingly by natural means but through fortuitous circumstances. The Magus himself may become the instrument for the fulfillment of his desire. Magic in action looks like luck. Magic should be used only when normal means of achieving desire are impossible, otherwise nothing will happen since the Magus will already possess the opportunity of accomplishing his intention.

Chapter 6

RUNE MAGIC

Rune magic has five distinct steps which are mentioned in the *Havamal*:

1. Cutting
2. Reading
3. Staining
4. Evoking
5. Sending

Cutting

In earliest times the runes, or symbols very much like the runes, were cut on wood with stone knives. For nomadic hunters of the forest, no material was more readily available than twigs of wood. They could be taken up or discarded at will. The knife was necessary for survival and would always be near at hand. Runes could be cut when the evening camp fire was made, then burned before the group moved on in the morning.

All magical materials are prepared with solemn ceremony in the sight of the gods and under their good auspices. Similar care must be taken with the runes. No doubt they were often care-lessly cut in ignorance or haste, but that a proper and accepted way of cutting them existed is probable. It may have varied in its details from tribe to tribe, but its purpose would remain the same—to set the runes apart from the mundane world and link them to a particular aspect of the spiritual world.

The wood upon which the runes are cut should be taken from a fruit-bearing tree. Nuts are considered fruits of the tree, so this includes such trees as the oak and chestnut. The branch is to be cut at a magically favorable time. The first light of dawn is suitable for honest works, symbolizing as it does the triumph of light over darkness. The vernal equinox, the moment the sun emerges from an eclipse, even the beaming of the sun's rays from behind a curtain of cloud have a similar significance. On the other hand, for works of evil the branch should be cut from a barren or dead tree in the darkness or shadow.

The knife used to lop off the bough, and later to cut the runes upon it, must be consecrated through a ceremony in which it is offered in service to the god or gods who will oversee the rune magic. If the knife is intended for general use it should be consecrated to all the gods who will act through it, or to the One who is over all. Odin in his guise as All-Father is an agent of the Nameless One, therefore the knife can be consecrated to the All-Father. Consecration usually takes the form of a prayer and a symbolic action such as the anointing with oil.

During the consecration of the knife, will the powers of the gods in whose names the knife will be used to flow into the blade. If you are able to clearly visualize the knife as gleaming and scintillating with radiance, its power will be greater.

The knife should be spotlessly clean and at least partially manufactured by the Magus—usually the hilt is made. It must be undamaged and unbroken, and preferably never employed for other than magical purposes. The blade must be razor sharp. An old knife in perfect condition can be used if it is thoroughly purified before consecration.

Purification is done by exposing the object to be cleansed to fire and water while speaking a cleansing prayer. Draw the blade through an open flame three times, moving it in a clockwise circle, so that it is warmed. Then sprinkle consecrated water over both its sides three times. An alternative is to dip the blade three times in a chalice filled with consecrated water.

The Magus seeks to glorify the gods, not insult them. He must never offer them anything he himself considers second rate. Since the gods look upon the instruments of the Art through his eyes, and his perception is modified by his prejudices, he must truly believe that his instruments are as perfect as he can reasonably make them.

Take a nine-inch long section of the branch and cut into its bark the runes to be used in the ritual. Allow the shavings to fall on the open ground, or if this is impossible gather them up and scatter them over tranquil earth. Cut each line of the runes with two sure and forceful strokes—the first to incise, the second to clear away the wood from the grooves. On a rounded wand this is best done with a slight rolling action.

The motions of the cuts should be from top to bottom and from left to right. Top to bottom is the line followed by the descending rays of the sun. Left to right is the path traced by the solar orb across the sky. Needless to say, in works of evil these directions are reversed.

Before beginning to cut the runes, speak an invocation to the god or gods who will oversee the ritual. It should be short and original, an invitation for the gods to take notice of your purpose and lend their authority to its fulfillment. Since the runes act independently, the gods invoked may be from any pantheon. For the unity of the ritual it is best to call upon the Teutonic gods when possible.

Runes can be formed with pen and paper. A pen nib is of steel and is used for marking a line in a way analogous to the cutting stroke of a knife. Modern paper is made entirely of new wood except at the extremes of quality—very cheap paper has recycled fiber; very expensive paper has a rag content. However when using pen and paper the tactile sensations of cutting the runes in wood, which are quite potent magically, are lost. The process of forming the runes becomes perfunctory and is liable to be undervalued.

Reading

At first consideration reading the runes might be interpreted simply as knowing what they mean. Any person using the runes for magic would know their names and associations. Why then list reading as a second step after cutting? Surely the two go together. And if they are considered apart, reading—or knowing what the runes signify—would naturally precede writing the runes down.

The explanation is that when a rune is read aloud it becomes actual in the mind and spirit. Speaking the rune carves it on the beating heart. Before it is spoken it exists potentially. Vibrated in the air by the lips and tongue, warmed by the breath of the lungs, it is born just as the universe was born at the Word of God.

Breath, air, words—all have powerful magical associations that transcend the boundaries of culture and time. Breath is the life force. Air is the medium of thought. Words are not mere symbols but living beings. By articulating the runes, the Magus lends each its unique identity that separates it from the undifferentiated mass of oblivion. He names them, and they awake with an awareness of their own being.

After the carving of the runes has been completed, they should be spoken aloud one after the other in order. The names need not be shouted. They may be barely audible to a nearby listener, but they must resonate inwardly. The Magus should receive the impression that they are spoken in peals of thunder. As he names each rune he forms an intellectual and emotional picture of it similar to the impression one gets on hearing the name of a familiar person.

There is a specific method for vibrating names in modern magic. Open your throat and allow the column of air in it to resonate against your diaphragm. This will produce a buzzing in the bones of the ears and a tickling in the nose. Your chest should vibrate like the skin of a drum. Each rune name is stretched out and fully articulated so that it seems to be spoken in slow motion.

The physical vibrations produced by this exercise must be transmitted into psychic channels so that they reach the higher spheres. The mechanics of vibration are only the means of effecting changes on the level of spirit. Of themselves they are powerless. Properly vibrating a rune name on all levels opens a communication with its secret essence and makes it available for use.

Staining

Originally runes were stained with blood; either the blood of the person using them, or the blood of a sacrificed human being or animal.

Berserkers (a name meaning bear coats) were a fanatical cult of Norsemen devoted to warfare who carved runes on their weapons and before a battle gashed themselves so that their blood flowed over the runes. They believed that the runes, particularly the Tyr rune, rendered them invulnerable. Their rage was similar to that of fanatical Moslems. They rushed into the thick of the fray without the least regard for their safety, and considered death by the sword a glorious honor as it assured them a place in Valhalla.

Grettis Saga in which the witch Duridr carves runes in the root of a tree and stains them with her own blood to bring ruin on Grettir, confirms that runes were bloodstained for reasons other than warfare. No doubt it was the common practice in all works of magic where much energy was required, but it is unlikely the blood always flowed from the veins of the sorcerer. It would be too great a temptation to take the easy way out and use the blood of a beast, fowl, or even another man.

The Romans mention human sacrifice among the northern tribes and there are echoes of it in the early writings of the Christian Church. For many years this was regarded as propaganda by Norse scholars who could not believe the hardy Vikings would descend to such acts, but not long ago physical evidence was uncovered, and there is now general agreement that human sacrifice was an occasional part of Teutonic worship. Very likely animal sacrifice was substituted early on as in other primitive cultures. A people that continues to sacrifice its members on a large scale cannot long endure.

Blood played the same role in rune magic as it plays today in Voodoo worship, where it acts as a source of supernatural nourishment and vitality, and is daubed upon an idol or spilled at its foot to feed the god. The most ignorant worshippers believe the idols to physically drink the blood, as they believe them to consume offerings of food and drink. More cultured worshippers look upon the physical blood as the outward manifestation of an invisible psychic blood which feeds the unseen and intangible spirits who dwell in the carven idols.

The truth is more subtle. Blood takes its vitality from the emotional and symbolic associations it has in the human mind. The gods or spirits feed on human feelings. This is why only blood spilled from the body of a worshipper will have full potency. A man may be indifferent to the spilling of animal blood. He may even be so depraved as not to react at the sight of a bleeding human being. In any case, his emotions will be more debased than those he experiences when his own lifeblood is shed.

To gain the maximum effect from the runes, the Magus must stain them with his own blood. As he cuts his skin and spreads his blood across the runes so that it settles into the grooves, he must not feel fear or regret. The self-shedding of blood is a voluntary sacrifice of the most intimate kind. It is at one moment a gift and a contract delivered to the rune powers. The Magus should fill his heart with quiet joy. It may help him to imagine the emotions of Odin hanging from Yggdrasill, or indeed of Christ on the cross.

Baser feelings such as lust, cruelty, fear, anger and hatred will evoke powers that are not only unproductive but dangerous. Sacrifice of another's blood can never produce the desired gestalt of psychic events, called a mind-state, dominated by a feeling of selfless surrender that is necessary for working constructive rune magic. No lasting pleasure can come from works of evil. What is first perceived as personal advantage swiftly turns to delusion and despair.

An ancient alternative to blood used to stain the runes was red ochre, an earth pigment. The Old English word *teafor* (pigment) is related to the Old Norse *taufr* (sorcery). Red ochre was rubbed along a rune staff in a powdered form to etch the lines of the runes against the background of the wood. Symbolically, it served as the blood of the earth.

The use of pigment is part of a process of degeneration in which the red blood of the magician became the blood of a human sacrifice, which became the blood of an animal, which became dried and powdered animal blood that need not be shed afresh each time magic was worked, which became red pigment linked to blood by color alone. The modern Magus should either go back to the source, his own fresh blood, or should follow the process to its logical conclusion and link in his mind red paint or ink to the emotions of sacrifice that alone feed the runes.

Blood will not necessarily work better than pigment. It depends on the mind-state the Magus is able to create and maintain. Blood is usually more effective only because it carries powerful natural associations. It is a psychological aid that the experienced Magus may not need to rely on.

However, do not fall into the modern error of thinking that since you recognize blood is a symbol, any other similar symbol will do as well. Symbols are alive. They each have a unique identity. They cannot be casually interchanged. An adept *may* be able to get the same results from red paint as he gets from blood, but it will require a highly developed mental control.

Blood is only one of the bodily fluids that may be used to stain the runes for different purposes. The others are saliva, urine, sweat, tears and semen (in women, menstrual blood). Each fluid carries unique associations and creates a different mind-state. For works of art or science, saliva is most effective. For works of destruction and storm, urine. For works of growth, sweat. For works of piety and love, tears. For sex magic, semen or menstrual blood.

Evoking

Evoking refers to the chants that are spoken over the runes to realize their power. Since the Germans had no literature, all incantations have been lost except for a few debatable scraps that may have survived in folk charms. By their nature the Norse chants were secret and never written down. Perhaps special gestures of the hands or body were used in conjunction with the chants, but these are a matter of speculation.

The chants must have been a summoning of the powers of spirits of the runes into manifest being; a calling of them from the potential to the actual. They were probably directed into the object upon which the runes were carved, or into the runes themselves. The rune object became the temporary home of the powers until they were sent to accomplish the desire of the shaman.

All magical chants are short, metrical, usually rhyming, and go straight to the point. They may be composed in the form of a riddle so that anyone overhearing them will not be able to guess their significance. Often they are repeated many times in a sing-song voice to induce a trance state so that their message will reach the subconscious. Rune chants will use the names of the Teutonic gods as words of power.

The chant should be accompanied by appropriate gestures designed to draw down the power of the runes, the most effective of which is the vortex. Revolve the knife over the runes in a sunwise circle while visualizing a psychic whirlwind whose center opens over them. Alternately, walk or dance around the runes set in the center of the magic circle sunwise. Nine revolutions should be made. Nine is a powerful number in rune magic and signifies realization.

Evocation has the effect of priming the runes. At this point the ritual may become dangerous. Previously the runes were empty markings on wood—now they are charged with occult potency. In addition to his other protective devices, the Magus should wear about his neck an amulet with the Eoh (ᛇ) rune prominently carved upon it. Before the runes are stained, the amulet should be stained. Before the forces of the runes are evoked, the protective power of the Eoh rune should be summoned into the charm. In this way if anything goes wrong with the ritual, the amulet will protect the Magus by the very powers that the rune spirits may try to use to harm him. Directions for making the amulet are found in the chapter on amulets and talismans.

Sending

Evoking and sending are closely related. In practice they may form two stages of a single action. However, they can be discussed separately. Evocation draws down the powers of the runes. Sending releases those powers toward the target. If evocation is thought of as loading and cocking a gun, sending is akin to aiming and firing.

Sending can be accomplished manually by passing the runes to another person or secreting them in a specific place. This method is imaginatively described in a story by M. R. James called *Casting the Runes*, in which a nigromancer takes a dislike to a critic and puts into his possession runes of destruction. The runes are timed to take effect at a certain hour. Throwing them away is no help—the only way the critic can save himself is by returning the runes personally to their maker, which he does just before the fatal hour by means of a trick.

When the runes cannot be delivered to the object of desire hand to hand or through the mail, they may be sent through the elements. All elements can be used with the exception of Light, which is too subtle, but one will be more appropriate in any given circumstance.

For example, if you wish the runes to act on a person who is aboard ship or to raise a tempest, the runes can be cast into the sea. If you wish to affect crops or property, the runes should be buried. If you desire to summon winds or otherwise change the weather, write the runes on a piece of paper and tear it into tiny pieces, then scatter them in the air. If you want to create emotional or physical heat, the runes are best burned.

Any method will work more or less well with any set of runes provided the proper concentration and visualization are linked with specific words of direction. Some elements are merely more appropriate for certain purposes. It can generally be stated that Fire is a suitable medium for works of war, lust, anger and violence; Air is fitted to works of science, philosophy, judgment and justice; Water is for works of love, art, kindness and illusion; and Earth is for works of construction, toil, strength and endurance.

Chapter 7

A COMPLETE RUNE RITUAL

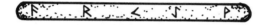

It may be difficult for someone not used to magical practice to translate the general instructions given in the preceding chapters into specific techniques. Here is a complete ritual of rune magic as a guide, not to be followed rigidly, but to be used as a starting point for more personal rituals.

Before beginning, undergo a period of purification and focusing. Memorize the ritual and prepare all the necessary materials. Make ready the ritual place. This ritual is designed to open a communication between the Higher Self and the ego. For maximum benefit it should be worked regularly, perhaps once a week for several months.

An hour or so before the ritual, bathe, drain the water from the tub and refill it with fresh water. Kneel before the tub and speak a prayer of cleansing over the water. As you pray, drop several grains of salt that have been previously consecrated into the water and bathe again. Dry yourself and don the ritual robe—a plain white garment that allows comfort and ease of movement. Go to the ritual place.

In the center of the place is the altar, which is about two feet square and waist high, its top covered with a white linen cloth. Place upon the altar the materials and instruments that have previously been prepared and consecrated. A candle in a short holder is set directly in the center of the altar top. Around it are arrayed a square of thin paper, a dip pen with a medium width nib, a bottle of red ink, a small chalice, a pitcher of clean water, an earthenware plate, and a sharp knife.

The rune amulet of protection is not needed in this ritual but may be worn about the neck if desired. Because the ritual invokes only the higher forces and is conducted within a magic circle, its dangers are minimal.

Glastonbury Tor, England.
One of the most famous pagan high places, where the sun was worshipped before the coming of Christianity. At one time an island that rose abruptly from the waters of the surrounding marsh, it was called by the Britons *Ynys yr Afalon,* and by the Romans Avallonia. King Arthur is reputed to be buried there.

Enter the place from the North, or if this is impossible, enter and proceed around the outer edge sunwise until you reach the North, then approach the altar and kneel. Light the candle. Close your eyes and try to empty your mind of thoughts and your heart of emotions. Strive for tranquility. Passively contemplate the task you are about to perform.

Clap your hands sharply together three times and lift them heavenward. Look past the flame into infinity. Speak the declaration of intent, which should go something like:

> **This ritual for the opening of the path of**
> **Light**
> **is well and truly commenced.**

Stand up and cross your body, touching with your right index finger your forehead, your groin, your left shoulder and your right shoulder. Touch your heart, then point directly at the flame on the altar. As you perform these gestures speak this prayer:

> **Thine is the Crown** (forehead)
> **And the Kingdom,** (groin)
> **The Power** (left shoulder)
> **And the Glory,** (right shoulder)
> **The Law everlasting;** (heart)
> **Amen.** (flame)

Pivot sunwise to face North. As you walk once sunwise around the altar, draw a circle with your extended index finger in the air at the level of your heart. The circle should be nine feet in diameter. Visualize it strongly as a blazing ring of white fire. It may previously be drawn on the floor with chalk or charcoal to aid in visualization. Take care to join the beginning with the end in your mind when you return to the North.

Inscribe in the air to the North with large gestures the Invoking Pentagram of Air. This is drawn from the point of Air clockwise with a continuous line. Visualize the pentagram in yellow flame. Point to its center and draw the Ger rune, which stands for Air, with downward strokes:

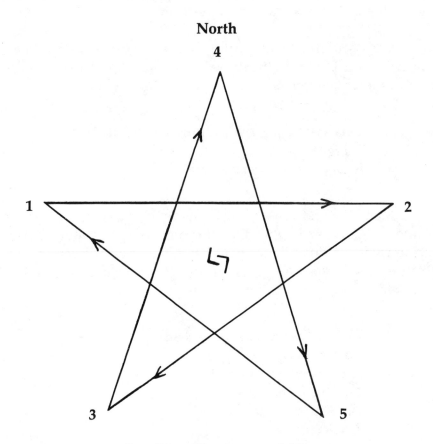

North

Invoking Pentagram of Air

Again pointing at the center of the pentagram, speak an invocation to the spirits of Air:

> *Spirits and powers of the wind,*
> *Attend and witness this ritual,*
> *Bear my wishes to the Nameless One,*
> *Open to me the path of Light.*

Go in a sunwise arc to the South and stand with your back to the altar. In the air to the South inscribe a large Invoking Pentagram of Fire. Visualize it in red flame. Point to its center and draw the Sigel rune, which stands for Fire, with downward strokes:

South

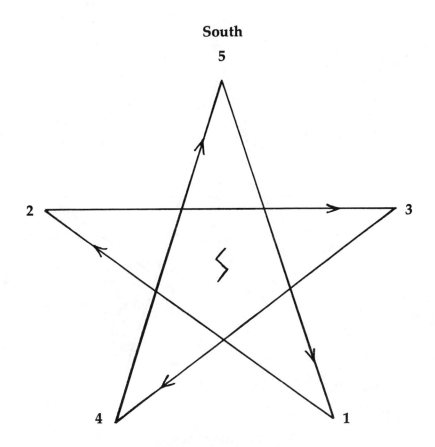

Invoking Pentagram of Fire

Pointing to the center of the Pentagram, speak an invocation to the Spirits of Fire:

> *Spirits and powers of the flame,*
> *Attend and witness this ritual,*
> *Bear my wishes to the Nameless One,*
> *Open to me the path of Light.*

Go sunwise around the altar to the East and draw in the air a large Invoking Pentagram of Earth. Visualize the pentagram in dark green flame. Point to its center and draw the Ethel rune, which is a symbol of Earth, with downward strokes:

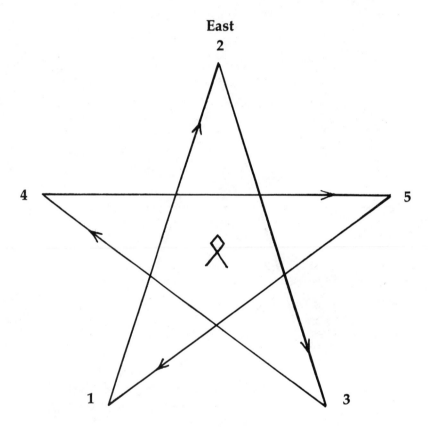

Invoking Pentagram of Earth

Pointing to the center of the Pentagram, speak an invocation to the spirits of Earth:

> *Spirits and powers of the furrow,*
> *Attend and witness this ritual,*
> *Bear my wishes to the Nameless One,*
> *Open to me the path of Light.*

Go in a sunwise arc to the West and draw outwardly in the air the Invoking Pentagram of Water. Visualize it of blue flame. Point to its center and draw the Lagu rune, symbol of Water, with downward strokes:

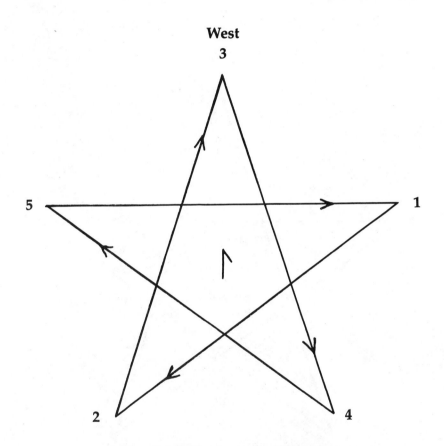

West

Invoking Pentagram of Water

Pointing to the center of the pentagram, speak an invocation to the spirits of Water:

> *Spirits and powers of the wave,*
> *Attend and witness this ritual,*
> *Bear my wishes to the Nameless One,*
> *Open to me the path of Light.*

Go sunwise in an arc to the North and face the altar. Draw in the air over the altar the Invoking Pentagram of Light, and within it the Ken rune, symbol of Light. The pentagram should be visualized as standing upright over the altar top and blazing with white flame:

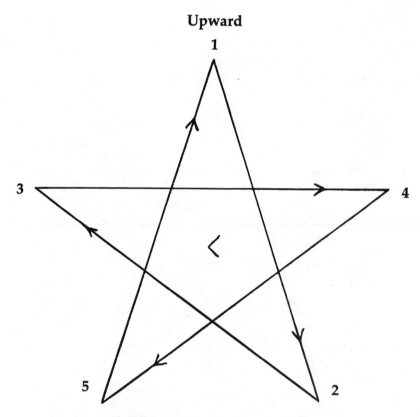

Invoking Pentagram of Light

Pointing to the center of the pentagram, speak an invocation to the spirits of Light:

Spirits and powers of the light,
Attend and witness this ritual,
Bear my wishes to the Nameless One,
Open to me the path of Light.

If these invocations to the elements are properly performed, the air around the circle will seem to pulsate and flicker, not so much visually as inwardly. You will feel a sense of watchfulness and waiting.

Still facing the altar, bring your legs together and spread wide your arms so that your body forms a great cross. Speak a prayer for centering yourself in the universe:

> *The Four surround me,*
> *The flames above, the waves below;*
> *I am the heart of the Four,*
> *I am the center of the universe.*

Bring your hands together in a prayer gesture over your heart. Visualize three beams of colored light intersecting your body. A red ray passes vertically through you from the crown of your head to the soles of your feet. A blue ray passes horizontally through your sides under your shoulders. A yellow ray passes horizontally through the center of your chest and out your back. Where the three rays intersect in your heart center, a white star blazes with dazzling brightness. Your praying hands clasp the beam of yellow light entering through your chest.

Begin to dance lightly around the altar in a sunwise direction. For every revolution you make about the altar, rotate on your own axis sunwise three times. Circle the altar three times, which will result in nine rotations. The spiral dance must be light and graceful—a gentle spinnning with your arms spread from your body. Take care not to lose your balance or bump the altar.

For each large circle speak a line of this verse:

> *Weave a circle round me thrice,*
> *Lift me from this earthly place,*
> *Show to me Thy holy face.*

The dizziness created by the spiral dance must penetrate the depths of your being. Visualize yourself upon a high place in the wilderness, a stone altar rising from the crown of the hill,

Odin by Fogelberg, Sculpture in marble.
On the helmet of the god are the crows Hagin (Thought) and Munin (Memory), and on his ankles wolfskins symbolizing his wolf familiars Geri and Freki. He holds the dwarf-forged spear Gungnir in his right hand.

trees stretching all around in a dark, unbroken carpet below, the stars of the night sky sparkling above.

Pivot and face the North with the altar behind you. Open your arms in a gesture of invitation. Visualize the god Tiw approaching the circle through the night air, his armor of silver and gold glinting with starlight, his blond hair streaming behind him, a sword in his single left hand. Speak his invocation:

> *Great and noble Tiw, the One-Handed,*
> *Lord of Justice, Lord of Oaths,*
> *God of airy reason and true speech;*
> *By thy sword I summon thee,*
> *By Fenrir's steel jaw I summon thee,*
> *By the Nameless One I summon thee,*
> *Descend into this circle and serve me.*

Go in a sunwise arc to the South and stand with the altar at your back. Open your arms in a gesture of invitation. Visualize the god Thor approaching through the night sky, his eyes showering sparks and his black hair writhing about his bluff, bearded face. He wears a bearskin, his magic girdle and magic gloves, and carries his great stone hammer in his right hand. Speak his invocation:

> *Strong and fierce Thor, the Thunderer,*
> *Lord of Battle, Lord of Works,*
> *God of mighty oaths and valiant deeds;*
> *By Thy hammer I summon thee,*
> *By Skrymir's glove I summon thee,*
> *By the Nameless One I summon thee,*
> *Descend into this circle and serve me.*

Go sunwise to the East and face outward, the altar at your back. Make the gesture of invitation. Visualize the god Frey approaching through the night sky, his body strong and well-proportioned, his long auburn hair tied in back of his head, his eyes a deep umber. He bears a wooden shield on his left arm. Speak his invocation:

Thor by Fogelberg. Sculpture in marble.

About the waist of the thunder god is his magic girdle, which doubles his strength. On his hands he wears the iron gloves needed to wield Mjolnir (the Destroyer), his great hammer, originally said to be made of a meteorite, perhaps because some meteorites are composed of an extremely hard and tarnish-proof nickel-steel alloy impossible to duplicate in ancient times.

> *Virile and potent Frey, the Renewer,*
> *Lord of Crops, Lord of Cattle,*
> *God of the green earth and the golden grain;*
> *By thy golden boar I summon thee,*
> *By Surt's stolen blade I summon thee,*
> *By the nameless One I summon thee,*
> *Descend into this circle and serve me.*

Go to the West in a sunwise arc and face outward. Make the gesture of invitation. Visualize the approach of Balder through the night sky, his light brown hair flowing in the breeze, his green eyes gentle and mild, his features delicate and his body slender. He wears embroidered robes and carries a golden horn. Speak his invocation:

> *Fair and beautiful Balder, the Beloved,*
> *Lord of Laughter, Lord of Cheer,*
> *God of clear light and loving heart,*
> *By thy prancing steed I summon thee,*
> *By Hod's cruel dart I summon thee,*
> *By the Nameless One I summon thee,*
> *Descend into this circle and serve me.*

Return to the North sunwise and face the altar. Make the gesture of invitation in the air over it. Look upward and visualize Odin descending from the sky, his great travel cloak billowing, his grey beard and long grey hair flying wildly behind him, his single grey eye glittering like ice. In his hand he carries his spear. Speak his invocation:

> *Wise and knowing Odin, the One-Eyed,*
> *Lord of Victory, Lord of Rule,*
> *God of magic and secret signs;*
> *By thy spear I summon thee,*
> *By Mimir's awful pledge I summon thee,*
> *By the Nameless One I summon thee,*
> *Descend into this circle and serve me.*

Kneel before the altar. Under the watchful eyes of the five great northern gods, write upon the paper with the pen and red

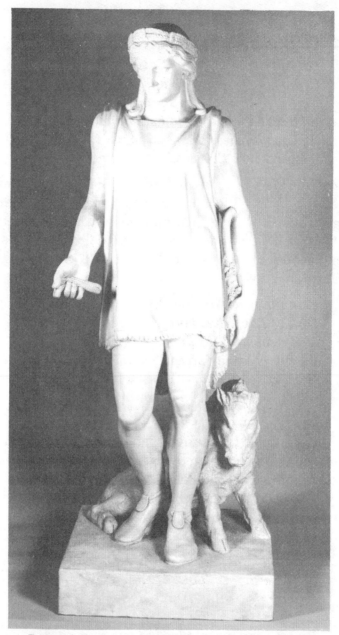

Frey with the Boar by Fogelberg. Sculpture in marble.
Beside the Vanir god stands the golden boar forged by dwarfs to draw his
chariot. On his head he wears a wreath of ripe grain, and carries what appears
to be a bundle of grain in his right hand. In his left hand he bears a leafy scep-
tre, symbol of fertility.

ink these runes:

In brief, they signify: man, horse, hardship, sacrifice, change, realization, sun, day, sun, glory, glory, glory.

Man and *horse* are the motive and the medium of seeking. *Need* is the suffering encountered on the quest. *Gift* is the voluntary letting go of care and the surrender to the higher will. *Cycle* is the change of fortune that then occurs. *Torch* is the light of awareness that dispels shadows. *Sun* is the light swollen to a powerful active energy for transformation. *Day* indicates the steadiness and completeness of the light—the two Sigel runes on either side of Daog show that the illumination can be used to bless or chastise. *Glory* is the blessing that follows the attainment of Light. It is threefold and thus perfectly balanced, divine, incorruptible.

After you have written the runes, vibrate them on your breath and cause the altar flame to flutter. You must hold the awareness of the total meaning of the combined runes clearly in your mind or the ritual will lack potency.

Take the knife in your left hand and pass its blade through the flame, then prick yourself on the ball of your right index finger until a drop of blood wells forth. Your feelings must be calm and joyful. You must welcome the twinge of pain and transmit it psychically to the gathered gods. Draw your finger across the runes from left to right. Allow a second drop of blood to fall into the chalice. If necessary, bandage the finger, but the cut should be so small it will soon stop of its own accord.

Lift the paper high over the altar and speak an invocation to the rune powers something like this:

> **Darkness into Light,**
> **Vice into Virtue,**
> **Lies into Truth,**

Balder by Fogelberg, Sculpture in marble.
He stands as a target for the weapons of the gods, which will not harm him, an arrow broken in his parted robe. An asp crawls mildly by his foot. In his hair are flowers, and perhaps leaves of mistletoe, foreshadowing his doom.

> *Pain into Joy,*
> *Weakness into Strength;*
> *By these runes transform me,*
> *Open my eyes and let me see.*

Lower the paper to the candle flame and light it on the corner, then place it on the earthenware plate. As the paper burns, put your hands close to it and lean over the altar so that its smoke rises to your face. Your hands should feel the heat of the flames. Inhale the rising smoke deeply without coughing.

After the paper has burnt to a fine ash, use the knife to reduce it to powder. Scrape the flakes of ash into the chalice, being careful not to miss any. Pour water from the pitcher over the ashes and the drop of your blood and stir all three together with the blade of the knife. Drink the mixture in the chalice to the last drop and turn the cup downward over the plate.

As you drink you should be able to feel the power of the runes coursing through your veins and causing your muscles to tremble. You may feel dizzy or lightheaded, and hear a loud rushing sound. Do not be fearful. Maintain an inner calm. This is the climax of the ritual to which all previous steps tended.

Do not expect to be immediately illuminated by this Elixir of Light. Its effect will be gradual and subtle, and may not begin to show itself for days or even weeks. Its action varies from person to person. Magic, like water, seeks the easiest route to the sea. Be assured, change will come. It is not always an easy transformation; you cannot realize how tightly you cling to your conceits until you feel yourself in danger of losing them.

The ritual is closed by reversing the order of the steps that opened it. Stand and make a warding off gesture with the splayed hands toward the air over the altar, as though pushing something away. Visualize the god Odin receding upward into the starry sky. Speak the banishment:

> *Wise Odin, depart in peace;*
> *By the Nameless One I license and compel*
> *thee.*

The banishment must be spoken in a firm and unequivocal voice with no trace of doubt in the mind or fear in the heart. Follow the departing god until he has completely vanished from your inner eye.

Go widdershins (against the course of the sun) to the West and banish Balder in a similar manner, using the appellation "loving" to describe him: "Loving Balder, depart in peace," etc. Go widdershins to the East and banish "Virile Frey." Go to the South and banish "Fiery Thor." Go to the North and banish "Noble Tiw."

Dance in a circle three times around the altar widdershins to seal the doorway open in your psyche, rotating widdershins on your body axis three times for each revolution of the altar. Speak one line of this verse for each great circle:

> *Weave a circle round me thrice,*
> *Turn from me Thy fearful face,*
> *Return me to my earthly place.*

You have now erased the vortex that allowed you to invoke the powers of the five gods. The next step is to neutralize the elemental powers you used in the ritual as conveyors of the virtues of the runes. Draw over the altar the Banishing Pentagram of Light, which is identical with the Invoking Pentagram but made in a counterclockwise direction. (See diagram next page)

Note that even the Ken rune in the center of the pentagram is drawn in reverse order with upward strokes. Since the rune was made last, it should be retraced first. As you trace each line, visualize it fading and vanishing from the air. Speak a simple banishment such as:

> *Spirits and powers of Light, depart in peace;*
> *By the Nameless One I license and compel*
> *thee.*

Upward

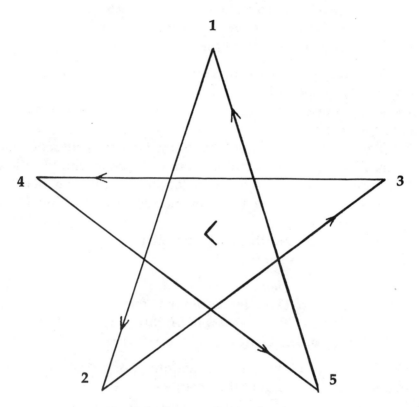

Banishing Pentagram of Light

Do the same for the other pentagrams of the elements, moving always in a widdershins direction. Go to the West, and facing outward, banish the spirits of Water; then go East and banish the spirits of Earth; then South to banish the spirits of Fire; and finally return North and banish the spirits of Air.

Facing the altar from the North, raise your hands and spread your fingers into two pentagrams. Extend your arms to the sides East and West at eye level. Speak a general banishing formula to all spirits that may be lingering outside the protective circle:

All spirits or entities attracted by this ritual,
Depart! For you have no lawful business here.
By the Light of the Nameless One, go!
Yet go in peace and fare thee well.

You must be certain that the space around the circle is empty of psychic influences before dissolving the barrier. If necessary, repeat the banishment more strongly using the gods as names of power.

The circle is erased by reabsorbing it into the center of your being. Walk once widdershins around the altar with your left index finger extended to touch the flaming circle. Visualize the white fire flowing into your left hand and vanishing from your perception.

Stand in the North facing the altar. Raise your arms to heaven. Speak this short prayer:

Holy art Thou, Father of All,
Holy art Thou, by Nature not formed,
Holy art Thou, Vast and Mighty One,
Lord of the Light and of the Darkness.

Cross your body as in the beginning of the ritual *without* reversing the direction of the gestures:

Who art the Crown (touch your brow)
And the Kingdom, (groin)
The Power (left shoulder)
And the Glory, (right shoulder)
The Law everlasting; (heart)
Amen. (point to the flame)

Speak the words of closing:

This ritual for opening the path of Light
is hereby well and truly ended.

Clap your hands sharply together four times. Blow out the candle and carefully clean and put away the instruments. Any residues of materials should be treated reverently and sealed with the sign of the circle-cross (⊕) before they are discarded.

Put away the instruments in a reverse order to that in which they were taken out.

Do not sleep directly after a ritual. Occupy the mind with some unrelated amusement. Avoid fretting or analyzing the effects of the ritual. If your mind is troubled, the ripples on its surface may prevent the ritual from taking proper effect. Very likely there will be aftershocks—troubling dreams, hypnagogic images, auditory and tactile hallucinations—but these should not persist longer than the first night after the ritual. If they linger, a simple banishing ritual will disperse them.

Chapter 8

AMULETS, TALISMANS AND SIGILS

The word amulet descends from the Old Latin *amuletum*, "means of defense." In ancient times it was used to describe any object, material or practice that had an avertive, protective or curative function. In modern use the word has come to mean a small object carried on the person, usually about the neck, that averts harm by magical means.

Talisman is from the Arabic root *talisan*, "to make marks like a magician." They are of many diverse sizes and shapes, not necessarily carried on the person. Talismans are created for aggressive as well as defensive purposes. Examples of talismans in Teutonic mythology abound. The falcon-feathered robe of Freyja that caused its wearer to fly through the air was a talisman, as was the dwarf-made ring Draupnir that constantly enriched its possessor.

Sigil is from the Latin *signum*, "sign." It is an emblem or signet expressing a magical intention, usually derived from a name or phrase either rigidly according to fixed methods or intuitively. Sigils embody occult power in their pattern and may be marked on any material. Runes are sigils, since each rune represents a name and an idea, and manifests its potency through its form, not by virtue of the object upon which it is carved.

In modern usage, the word talisman is a broad term describing an instrument for working magic, and contains within it the notion of amulets. Sigils may be marked on both talismans and amulets to increase their efficacy, but are not strictly necessary to either. For example, certain natural stones without markings of any kind have been used as amulets by many cultures.

Runes can be placed on significant objects to make both amulets and talismans. In these cases, part of the working force is from the runes, part from the shape of the object, and part from the material of which the object is formed. Also, magical energy can be infused into otherwise nonmagical substances through a ritual act of will.

Consider the magic wands unearthed by researchers. These are short staffs of yew or bone, straight or curved in the shape of a horn or tusk, with runes carved on their sides. Some of their magical effectiveness would stem from the runes, some from the material, some from the horn shape, and perhaps some from the infused purpose of their creators. No one is certain how these wands were used. If they were carried on the person for protection they would be called amulets. However, if they were used for active magic, they would better be termed talismans.

Rune sigils can be formed quite easily by treating the runes as letters and combining them in magically appropriate geometric patterns. The exact final pattern selected is a matter of intuition, which insures that the sigils are actively linked to the subconscious. A spirit name or indeed any word that signifies a desired magical action is converted into rune letters, which are then compressed and doubled up into an emblem of the name.

This system of sigil making has a long history. Below is the sigil of the angel Raphael taken from a medieval grimoire called the *Enchiridion*:

Raphael becomes—

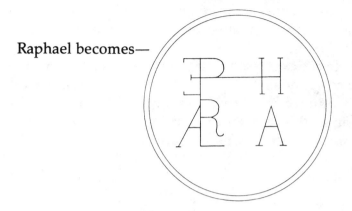

The number of possible combinations that can be formed is infinite, but reflection and intuition will select one pattern from the rest that seems more appropriate than the others. Several sigils of each name should be made, and the most pleasing chosen from among them. The Magus should receive an inner sense of its rightness when looking upon the final selection. If it is not completely satisfying, discard it and continue trying different patterns until the right one represents itself.

Sigils can be made from the names of the Teutonic gods. For example, Thor when converted into runes becomes ↑ᚺ᛭ᚱ . This can be patterned into the sigil shown below:

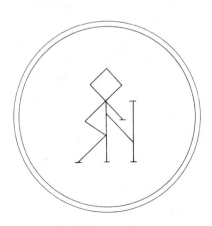

Any magical desire that can be expressed in a phrase can be reduced to a word by combining the significant first letters of each word in the phrase. The word thus created is the magical name of the desire expressed through the phrase. When converted to runes, a rune sigil can be made from it. For example the phrase "Odin bring the rain" can be reduced to O + B + R. Converted into runes, this yields the magical word ᛩᛒᚱ which can be transformed into the following sigil:

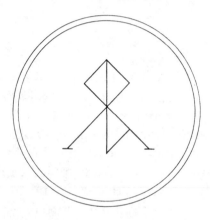

Compression of two or more runes into a single character is an ancient practice. Runes that shared elements in common were called bind runes. ᚺᚠ was sometimes written ᚻ and ᛘᚱ became ᛉ . Sometimes variants developed to distinguish these joinings: ᛘᛈ was written ᛂ . Runes were probably bound together to increase the ease with which they could be carved into stone. Each line of stone carving requires considerable effort; where the carver could make a single stroke serve two letters it was to his advantage.

A great virtue of runes is that they can be carried in the head and made without special tools or materials anywhere. Scratching or staining the Eolh rune upon a shield converted it into an amulet of protection. Tyr incised on the blades of swords made them into talismans of power, unbreakable and invincible. A Nyd rune cut upon the nail of the hand warned a warrior in the mead hall that his cup was poisoned.

Permanent rune amulets can be made in the skin itself by tattooing various parts of the body. Historically, runes were scarred or tattooed on the chest and hands. Simply by cutting the skin under the runes and muttering an invocation, their power could be released. Less permanent body amulets were formed of pigment. When Caesar landed in Britain, he reported that the natives painted their bodies blue with a dye called *woad*—a word perhaps connected with Woden, an earlier variant of Odin.

In an emergency, runes can be scratched into the breast with the fingernail. A red welt will rise up in the shape of the runes and a small amount of bleeding will occur that will feed the runes. At the same time the runes should be read and evoked. When the mind has been previously conditioned to accept the influence of rune forces, this method is quite effective.

Talismans can be made by painting the runes with food dye on bread, cake or biscuit and consuming them to realize their power. Bread is the best medium. Paint the runes on white bread with red food coloring using a medium-fine brush. Lightly toast the bread. It can then be cut into a significant number of pieces and ritually eaten before the altar.

The rationale for eating the runes is the same one behind the Christian practice of eating wafers said to be the body of Jesus: a desired power or virtue is transferred to the edible substance, then taken in by the mouth. The mouth is the symbolic gateway to the true Self. Through it the secrets of the mind are spoken. Through it the foods that sustain life are ingested. Passing the runes between the lips represents breaking the barrier everyone erects around their innermost being.

An amulet for general personal protection should be made by anyone who proposes to practice rune magic. The gods and spirits of the runes are unpredictable and often violent in their actions. They are not forgiving of stupidity. They always exact payment for their services. The onus is on the Magus to see that the payment he gives is of his own choosing.

An explicit warning of the dangers inherent in rune-craft is given in the *Havamal*:

Better not to ask than to overpledge,
as a gift demands a gift,
better not to slay than to slay too many.

This means better not to ask anything of the runes than to ask what will require you to pledge in payment more than you are freely prepared to lose. Any service from the runes to man must always be balanced by a service of equal value from man to the runes. When you work runes to bring disaster on your foes, take care you do not inadvertently harm your friends, because once awakened the powers of the runes are hard to control.

The amulet of protection is made from a chip of oak about three inches square and one-quarter-inch thick. It is hung about the neck with the grain of the wood running transversely. Wool, linen, cotton, silk or any synthetic can be used for the cord, but only use leather that has been ritually purified.

On the front, mark the Eolh rune largely so that it fills the face of the amulet. On the back write in runes the word *alu*— protection. Carve above it the symbol of Thor's hammer, the swastika, rotating in a clockwise direction with its arms trailing. The clockwise swastika is a symbol of positive solar action. Beside the swastika, carve the rune sigil of your magic name. In the example given below the name Sunchild has been used to form the sigil pictured on the amulet:

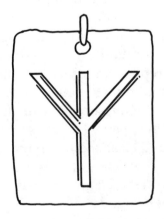

Front

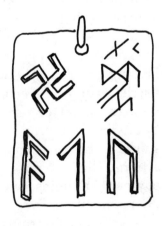

Back

The magic name markes the death of the earthly life and the resurrection on the path of Light. It is given after a ceremony of initiation by the leaders of the occult group into which the initiate gains admittance. If a self-initiation is conducted, the initiate must seek his or her own name through inspiration, by meditating and invoking the Light. Once received, the name must never be divulged to another as it embodies the magical power of the Magus at that particular stage in his or her evolution.

The amulet will possess no protective power until it is consecrated and energized through a ritual in which the Eolh rune is traced over in the blood of the person whose name appears on the back, and the powers of the gods—particularly Balder—are invoked. Then if the amulet falls into the hands of another person, it will not protect them since it is inextricably linked to its maker.

Wear the amulet at all times during serious or difficult rune magic, and stain it afresh whenever particularly great magical forces are called forth. It is a good idea to get into the custom of putting it on before every ritual—its presence cannot hurt and may help in the event of unforeseen difficulties. When not in use it must be kept in a safe place, never seen except by other initiates; never touched by anyone. The Magus should arrange for it to be destroyed in the event of his or her death.

Runes can be combined in talismans with other magical symbols. Especially useful are the signs of the elements, planets, Zodiac and Geomancy. I Ching hexagrams can be used by those who well understand them. The power of the runes can be further defined and directed through the use of appropriate colors, shapes, materials, and by making the talisman on a specific day and hour that is astrologically auspicious.

There is a point of diminishing returns in making talismans when the difficulty of forming increasingly subtle correspondences is greater than any possible good they accomplish. All talismans are necessarily imperfect. They should be constructed simply, using a few of the most potent and appropriate symbols.

Loading them with every imaginable magical symbol will decrease, not increase, their efficacy.

In ancient times the entire rune alphabet was thought to possess its own talismatic power. Several examples of complete or almost complete alphabets have been unearthed, the most famous of which is the Thames scramsax—a sword found in the river Thames near London in 1857. On the sword is inlaid with brass and silver wire the full 28 characters of the Old English rune alphabet and the name of the sword, or its maker.

Thames Scramasax. Iron with brass and silver inlay. 9th century.
Dredged up from the bottom of the River Thames in 1857, this is one of the most significant rune artifacts. It bears the entire early 28 character Anglo-Saxon *futhorc*, along with the name *Beagnoth*—probably the name of the sword.

It may be that this was only a mnemonic device, but more probably the alphabet symbolized the powers of the runes united in potential and waiting to be called forth. A similar talisman can be made more easily and compactly by combining all the strokes of the rune letters one over the other. Each rune is made of only two simple components, a vertical and a diagonal line. When the alphabet is overlaid this symbol results:

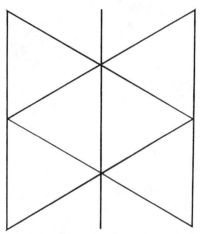

The combined symbol can fulfill the talismatic function of the collective rune alphabet. Those familiar with the Kabbalah will notice that the points on the glyph are ten, and that they fall upon the Sephiroth in the so-called restored Tree of Life, where Malkuth has been elevated to the position of Daath. Runic and Kabbalistic magic are compatible.

When making amulets and talismans, or using the runes for sigils, care must be taken that the magic meaning of the runes does not conflict with the letter meaning. Runes can be used merely for a decorative script but it should not be expected that they will convey any potency in this role. Straightforward transliteration will bring them together arbitrarily, causing them to neutralize each other. They will of course still convey the power of the words they represent, as would any script.

On the ancient rune amulets, a compromise was reached between the scriptural and magical meanings of the runes. The amulets often contain both intelligible words and a string of

Hammer of Thor. Silver pendant.
In addition to its function as a weapon, the hammer of Thor was used to consecrate treaties and marriage contracts. A magical amulet with avertive power.

gibberish that philologists have been unable to decipher. The words are the scriptual content of the amulet—they convey pertinent information such as the name of the maker, the name of a god, words of power and the purpose for which the amulet is intended. The gibberish, which is really not gibberish at all, is the magical content. These runes are used as symbols rather than letters. They are the magical heart of the amulet. The script runes define and direct the magical power; the symbol runes embody it.

The secret language of magic is numerical, as the Greek philosopher and mystic Pythagoras observed thousands of years ago. It is based on the meaning created when elements are brought together in patterns. The patterns, or magical words, are more than the sum of their parts. Their meanings may be simple or very complex—a human being is a word spoken by God.

In writing magically the Magus imitates, crudely and inaccurately, the speech of God. He or she takes numbers and their aggregates and forms words with the conviction that if he or she can only attain a sufficient accuracy the words will spring to life. The literature of magic is written on the world. It is in the pattern of the stars and the shape of a tree. It is in the way a drop of dew slips from a leaf and falls into a pond, and the shining framework of a spiderweb.

No one can teach magical writing. It must be intuited. But it is everywhere, even in the simplest thing. It can only be read with the eye of the Spirit. To the outer sight it appears a mere chance arrangement of elements. Advice given by mystic Masters to their students is that they take themselves apart and contemplate some simple object—a stone, a stick, a flower. Since all magic in the world is written in the smallest grain of sand, silence and a passive opening of the mind can sometimes let in the Light.

Here are the general magical meanings of the first twelve numbers. It must be stressed that they can only be fully apprehended when the heart and the head act together:

One rune signifies creation and beginning; the all enclosed in the One; birth.

Two runes indicates a balance of forces; the male and female; all dualities. The balance can be harmonious or conflicting.

Three runes signifies completeness and perfection, the runes functioning on the level of the ideal.

Four runes indicates that their power is expressing itself materially. This number is linked with the four lower elements.

Five runes indicates the presence of human will which may be either productive or destructive. This number is linked to man.

Six runes come under the sway of the Nameless One, who is the One in All and the All in One. Blending of opposites.

Seven runes suggests a supernatural function and matters concerning spirits and miracles. This number is linked to the planets.

Eight runes signifies frustration and suspension of action. It is a compound magically, as are all the numbers that follow. Four opposed to four; one material result confronts another.

Nine runes are under heavenly order and the rule of law, where effects follow causes. Nine is a compound of three times three and is considered the most perfect number.

Ten runes indicate the beginning of a new cycle, and therefore the material realization of the old cycle. Ten is a compound of nine plus one. However, it can also be read as five plus five, and in this guise it suggests man opposing man.

Eleven runes occur in works of evil. Eleven is a compound of nine plus two; that is, perfection reflected or inverted. Viewed as five plus six it is man confronting God. Always an evil number.

Twelve runes signifies the marriage of heaven and earth. Twelve is a compound of three times four, and also four times three; that is, matter made perfect and spirit made concrete. A favorable number for all good works. This number is linked to the Zodiac.

Chapter 9

SKRYING AND ASTRAL TRAVEL

Each rune symbolically represents a force in nature and a quality of the human soul. When used rightly, runes can affect the subjective inner world of thoughts and feelings, and the outer objective environment. Both are one from the magical viewpoint. The barrier between inside and outside is an artificial wall erected at the time of humanity's fall. By liberating the Higher Self from its bondage to the flesh, the Magus can transcend the bar across the gate of Eden and perceive the underlying unity of things. This perception is the key to power.

The potency inhering in each rune is given a concrete form by the workings of the mind. The mind will give the rune a form whether the ego wills it or not, but the form of the rune can in some measure be modified by deliberate intervention. This actualization of the rune identity is twofold and reflects the duality of microcosm and macrocosm.

The microcosmic form is a spirit which exhibits by its gestures, movements, appearance and voice the qualities of the rune it represents. It is usually humanoid, but may take the shape of an animal, a monster, or even an elemental presence.

The rune spirit will not be perceptible to the outer eyes except under extraordinary conditions such as mental illness, ritual exhaltation or extreme stress. It will relate to the Magus on a personal level, as one self-aware being to another, and may try through persuasion or intimidation to exert an authority over the Magus.

The macrocosmic form is a landscape, house, cave or other environment perceived by the Magus to be larger than his ego-envelope. He may look upon the rune world from a distance as through a window or the lens of a telescope; or he may find himself plunged into its setting. The rune world reflects the nature of the rune through its climate, geography, flora and fauna. It may be inviting or distressing.

Rune spirits and rune worlds can occur together. Walking in a rune world, it is not uncommon to encounter the ruling spirit, who is a petty lord over the forms that subsist there. It should be understood that the inhabitants of a rune world are not real in the material sense; neither are they unreal. Rather they are devices of the mind to communicate more effectively with the underlying potency of the rune.

Created by the mind, the mind has sovereignty over them, but not the ego. The conscious mind may hold the desire to formulate a rune spirit or rune world. It does not do the actual forming. Although the conscious mind may seek to command the spirit, or change the world, it cannot do so without the concurrence of the subconscious, which is brought into play through the use of symbols.

The rune symbol, when properly understood, invokes the potential of the rune. It gives the Higher Self acting through the subconscious a pattern upon which to mold a portion of the limitless, amorphous vitality of the Unmanifest into something that can be recognized and experienced. The intuited significance of the rune symbol guides the inner mind in casting a particular shadow on the infinite Light. This created form can only be commanded by the higher consciousness that created it. The ego of the Magus can at most direct the Higher Self with symbols, acting through the subconscious.

This explains the importance of purity. Purity is a heightening of awareness of the Higher Self. The Magus cleanses himself that he may gain power. It happens that this power is only obtainable by approaching the will of God. Building on a base of physical cleanliness, he seeks to purify his thoughts and emotions by focusing the Will on his highest destiny.

Ritual opens the psychic doors that purity unlocks. In skrying, these doorways are merely looked through. In astral travel, the ego passes into the secret chambers of the psyche, each of which contains its own world. Astral travel is the more seductive and dangerous of the two activities. In skrying, the inner world is held at arm's length and remains merely a picture: very lifelike, entrancing, perhaps frightening, but still only an image. In astral travel, the illusion envelops the ego and floods in through all the senses. It is difficult to cling to the comforting belief that it is an inner, not an outer, reality when it exists vibrant and alive on all sides.

Both skrying and astral travel are conducted in a silent dimly-lit environment of neutral temperature, safe from the possibility of interruption. Ritual robes should be worn, or if none are available, simple loose clothing. Before beginning, surround yourself with a circle of protection. Sit in the circle on a cushion or mat with your back straight and your shoulders relaxed. It is important that your lungs and internal organs not be compressed by slouching. You should practice sitting until you can sit effortlessly for at least half an hour. Any tendency to fidget will destroy the necessary concentration.

Skrying and astral travel are the same process at root. In skrying, the formal fiction of separateness from the vision is maintained. This is mechanically reinforced by using an instrument in which vision inheres. Popular media for skrying include mirrors, water, ink, crystal balls, polished metal surfaces, smoke, embers, hanging fabrics, and similar featureless materials. The important factor is that they provide no point of distraction for the eye. Such materials possess no power in themselves but act as backdrops for the inner sight.

Undirected skrying yields random visions. Whatever is uppermost in the psyche comes to the surface. When a symbol with a specific meaning is used as a focus, a vision directly linked to it arises in a trained mind that refuses to allow itself to be distracted. Just as some adepts can cause particular dreams, so can they cause particular visions.

A small mirror about a foot square is a good instrument with which to begin. Set it on a low table, or upon the altar if a magic temple is being used, and draw a circle around yourself. You can safely include the mirror since the circle takes in only the mirror itself, not the visions that appear in its depths. The mirror acts as a window in the wall of the magic circle.

Stand the mirror vertically so it will be at eye level when you are seated and about four feet away from your face. The room should be in almost total darkness with only the fuzzy outlines of larger objects discernible. It is important that no reflections are visible in the mirror. Sit comfortably. Strike a match or lighter, and with the flame draw the shape of the rune you wish to skry in the air before the mirror. Close your eyes while moving the flame from the end of one stroke to the beginning of another.

The afterimage of the flame will linger for several minutes on your retinas and you will see the shape of the rune, which you must concentrate on with all your Will. At the same time your mind must be empty of thoughts. Simply regard the rune with acute attention. As the image fades, look through and beyond it.

A greyish shimmering area will form in the depths of the mirror. It may be quite small at first, sometimes no larger than the central part of the palm of your hand, but it will grow until it covers most of the mirror surface. It will begin to churn and sparkle. Brief flecks of intense light may appear. As the grey zone clears, an image will form that seems very far off, as though you were looking at it through the wrong end of a telescope. If you do nothing to disturb it, the image will strengthen and draw nearer.

You must not study the image consciously or it will disappear. It emanates from a reflective state of mind. Once the mind becomes active, the image will retreat back into the depths of the subconscious. Contemplate the image passively and allow it to involve your attention. Anyone who has tried to look at a faint star in the night sky will understand. If you look directly at the star it vanishes; if you look slightly to one side you can see it, but only so long as you do not focus your eyes upon it. The same is true of skrying; only instead of averting the eyes you must avert the mind.

Sometimes you will see in the mirror the rune world from high in the air as though you were flying over it. The image will focus on a particular scene and you will seem to descend. A face may appear that fills the mirror. This is the rune spirit, who will answer your questions if you prove that you carry the authority of the Light. You should ask the magical name of the spirit so that on future occasions you can summon it at will.

It is a good idea to compose two incantations, *one for opening the mirror and another for sealing it shut.* That way you can better control the process of skrying. It would be inconvenient if you began seeing visions every time you looked at some shiny object with a contemplative gaze. This is the fate of the uncontrolled trance medium. A Magus will not permit the intrusion of astral images when he or she does not seek them.

For astral travel, a related but somewhat different technique is used. The mirror should be full length and the light in the ritual chamber slightly brighter. Paint the rune you intend to travel into on a small card and wear it about your neck. Draw a circle of protection around yourself and the mirror. Again, the mirror is the aperture through the wall of the circle, but this time it functions as a doorway rather than a window.

Sit facing the mirror about six feet away. Fix your attention on the reflected image of the rune about your neck. There should be just enough light to see it. At the same time imagine that you are your image, and your image is you; that you have traded places with the form in the looking glass. The rune about your neck will seem to waver and glow, and may become larger. Everything else will grow indistinct.

When you have convinced yourself that you are looking out from the inside of the mirror at your physical body, close your eyes but keep the image of the rune distinct in your mind. In your imagination stand up and draw with your right index finger the rune sigil of your magic name on the inner surface of the glass. It will act as a barrier to any extraneous forces that might try to gain access to the circle and your body while you are absent. Turn and walk into the world of the rune.

The scenery around you will echo your conception of the nature of the rune about your neck. It may differ from your conscious expectation, for the subconscious and conscious do not always agree. Everything will be colored by the character of the rune. To test the validity of the landscape, draw the rune largely in the air before you. The scene should brighten but otherwise be unchanged. If it is false and not related to the rune it will waver and darken, and be replaced by another more appropriate vision.

The land of the rune is not empty but filled with an infinite variety of beings. As you meet them, salute them with the rune sign, which will let them know that you are there lawfully. Before long you will encounter the ruling entity of the rune world, called the rune spirit. Salute it with the rune sign with a courtesy that befits its position, however do not humble yourself before it since you are a son or daughter of the Nameless One and its lawful master. Ask the spirit its magic name if you do not already know it.

You can converse with these beings on matters that come under the province of the rune and they will give you answers according to their power. Their desire to please and seem important in your eyes will sometimes outweigh their ability to give you accurate information. Examine their comments critically and disregard any assertions that conflict with reason. Occasionally the rune spirit may seek to deliberately mislead you. If you suspect deception you can test its veracity with the names and sigils of the High Gods and Goddesses.

As you walk through the rune world with your questions unspoken in your mind, there will arise tableaus and dumb shows designed to give you insights into your problems. These are much the same as dreams in that they seem arbitrary yet can be related to internal conflicts. The benefit derived from astral pantomimes will depend on your powers of analysis and introspection when you come to reflect on them after the astral journey is completed. Remember, everything you see is intended for your consideration. Disregard nothing.

When you wish to return to the mirror doorway you can retrace your steps, or simply will yourself to be back where your journey began. There is never a danger of becoming lost in the world of the rune. Its inhabitants may attempt to intimidate and confuse you, but ultimately your Will is law. The rune world has been formed by your desire acting through your Higher Self—it can just as easily be dissolved into nothingness.

The only danger that can arise during astral travel is when you forget your identity and begin to merge with the rune world. As long as you perceive yourself as standing in your normal human body, experiencing the scene through your human senses, you are safe. It is often a temptation to take on other forms, or simply let your awareness fly like an eagle over the land of the rune. This should be avoided. Whenever you feel yourself drifting into the vision or being overwhelmed by the astral environment, focus your will powerfully on being once more in your physical body, and no astral barrier can obstruct your return.

In the normal course of astral travel, you will return to your flesh more gently. Reach out your left hand and touch the rune sigil of your magic name that still glows on the inner surface of the mirror. Imagine it flowing back into your body. It will fade and disappear from the glass. Then sit down facing outward in the same position as your physical body. Will yourself to be looking into the mirror from the outside at your reflected image. Open your physical eyes. You will be once more sitting in your body facing the mirror.

This is only one of many methods of astral travel. It requires a fairly high degree of visualization and inner control. Some adepts prefer to travel while their bodies are in a reclining position so that they can allow the astral vision to pass gently into natural sleep. The disadvantage of this method is the tendency to lose awareness and with it the power to control the astral world. While it is true no physical harm can result from astral travel, mental difficulties may arise if the rune world is permitted to escape from conscious control. You may find yourself entering astral landscapes against your wishes.

At first, skrying and astral travel will be largely a matter of wishful thinking as you try to force yourself to perceive your preconception of the rune world. Then when you learn not to try so strenuously, but rather to let yourself receive impressions as they arise, the wish will become the inner reality.

Below is an example of the type of world and spirit you may encounter when you travel into each of the 24 Germanic runes. As has been pointed out, rune visions are subjective and will differ according to the individual understanding of the runes.

1. *FEOH* is a medieval agrarian community with a squalid village of about two dozen huts outside the walls of a castle. Everything has a dismal, soiled look. The people walk with their heads bowed.

   The spirit of Feoh is the overseer, a great bulk of a man with a bellowing voice and a whip. He is filthy, his black hair matted, his eyes blinking with stupidity.

2. *UR* is a primal forest filled with wild beasts that constantly battle. Its people are stealthy, silent hunters with sly eyes. They paint their naked bodies to blend into the undergrowth.

   The spirit of Ur is a hunter who carries a spear and wears a mask made of the head of a bear. He seldom speaks, but gestures.

3. *THORN* is a great cavern with a sulphurous lake from which fire belches. It is inhabited by scaley, crawling things that lurk in the darkness.

   The spirit of Thorn is a dragon-like monster. Its massive

head is serpent-like, black and wreathed in smoke and shadow.

4. *OS* is a landscape of rolling wooded hills with white-capped mountains rising in the distance. In its midst is a hall formed from the bodies of living trees with many fantastic carvings on its sides.

   The spirit of Os is an old chief with grey hair dressed in armor who sits at the head of the table in the hall and rules the land wisely.

5. *RAD* is a long road that winds between barren cliffs and impenetrable forests. Along it move silent, weary riders and people with bundles on their backs.

   The spirit of Rad is a strolling minstrel and storyteller who dresses in bright colors and entertains his fellow travelers.

6. *KEN* is a land of crystal and glass. The glass trees bear jewels as fruit and the sky is lit with rainbow colors that pulsate and make the landscape dance.

   The spirit of Ken is a woman surrounded by light who floats like a flame over the mirror surface of the earth. Her voice makes the crystal trees ring with mellow tones.

7. *GYFU* is a land of blood and destruction inhabited by people who have committed various acts of self-mutilation similar to those practiced by Indian fakirs.

   The spirit of Gyfu is a blind man bound to the trunk of a great tree.

8. *WYN* is a shining mountain that rises into a golden cloud. Near the top is a city of white stone. Its people are gentle and contemplative.

   The spirit of Wyn is a woman of slender build and blond hair. She wears white and speaks with a musical voice.

9. *HAEGL* is a blowing storm of hail and snow in a dark

evergreen forest.

The spirit of Haegl is not seen, but can be heard moaning and roaring on the wind.

10. *NYD* is a narrow wooden bridge across a chasm of foaming rapids. The center of the bridge is burning.

The spirit of Nyd is a horrifying but uncertain shape that threatens from behind.

11. *IS* is a frozen lake in winter. From the lake rises a small island overgrown with naked willows.

The spirit of Is lives on the island. Her appearance changes and allures. Sometimes she is beautiful; other times her face twists with hatred. She keeps a white owl.

12. *GER* is a flour mill beside a stream. It is dominated by a giant water wheel that turns and groans continuously.

The spirit of Ger is a robust man with a red face and a balding head. He wears a flour-covered leather apron and carries a cup of water and a wooden mallet.

13. *EOH* is a field of battle on the eve of conflict. Banners fly. Campfires burn. Men and horses wait for dawn and look silently across the darkened field at the fires of the foe.

The spirit of Eoh is a stocky foot soldier with a bow slung on his back, unkempt hair and dark eyes. His speech is crude but honest.

14. *PEORD* is a glade of apple trees where an abundance of fruit and other harvest goods have been gathered. Long tables set with plenty entertain the harvesters.

The spirit of Peord is a noble woman who oversees the feast and goes from table to table pouring wine from a pitcher she carries on her shoulder.

15. *EOLH* is a great gate set across a road between two rock cliffs. No passage is possible except through the gate. Many

people wait on the outside to gain admittance.

The spirit of Eolh is the unseen gatekeeper who lives over the gate. His voice is deep and threatening. He rains down fire and sword blades on those who try to approach.

16. *SIGEL* is a land so blazing with light that no details of it can be distinguished. The air roars with the sound of flames.

    The spirit of Sigel is never met directly. He communicates through proud emissaries who speak and receive replies.

17. *TYR* is the midst of a battle on a misty field. Usually only the clash of swords and the cries of the dying can be heard. Sometimes a pair of combatants come into view for a brief moment through the mist.

    The spirit of Tyr is a silent figure with a drawn sword who stalks the field ghostlike and chooses those who are to die. He communicates with gestures. His face is veiled.

18. *BEORC* is a glade of birch trees seen in the slanting sunlight of early morning. Birds sing. A clear spring bubbles.

    The spirit of Beorc is a girl who plays among the trees. She keeps a full grown stag as a pet.

19. *EH* is a grassy plain stretching endlessly to the horizon. On it move herd animals, particularly wild horses.

    The spirit of Eh is a young boy dressed in rabbit skins with wild eyes and long blond hair who rides a white stallion by clinging to its neck and lacing his fingers in its mane.

20. *MAN* is the inside of a house with uncounted corridors and rooms. Each room presents a different dramatic tableau.

    The spirit of Man is the holder of the keys. He is unseen but leaves an occasional door open.

21. *LAGU* is the depths of the sea-green ocean. Its inhabitants

dwell in the rocks and strange growths on the ocean floor. They are of monstrous appearance.

The spirit of Lagu is a mermaid with bluish skin. She sings songs that evoke illusions.

22. *ING* is a small but prosperous farm with a stone and thatch house and a wattle barn. Its inhabitants are the members of a family—grandfather, father, mother, a son who is nearly grown, a younger daughter, and an infant. They extend hospitable welcome to strangers.

The spirit of Ing is the grandfather, an elderly but hardy man with snow-white hair, who knows much lore of nature.

23. *DAEG* is a stone pillar that marks the passage of the sun. From it extend twelve spokes made of ridges of earth to the horizon. The sun never sets, but rides in an unending circle around the sky.

The spirit of Daeg is a bird with shining multicolored wings who perches atop the pillar of the sun wheel.

24. *ETHEL* is a geometric land where separate farms are arranged in a checkerboard pattern. Each small holding has a high fence around it.

The spirit of Ethel is the surveyor who determines the lay of the boundary lines. He walks the land continuously measuring the ground with a long rod as he goes.

Chapter 10

ABOUT DIVINATION

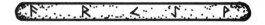

Runes can be used to peer into the future and to search out hidden things, but in order to divine rightly it is necessary to understand the forces that are at work.

All divination depends on a cardinal principle of magic that is stated most cogently in the Smaragdine, or Emerald Tablet, of Hermes Trismegistus:

> What is below is like that which is above; and
> what is above is like that which is below.

This is perhaps the single most potent statement ever made, rivaling even the "Know Thyself" of the Greeks. Unfortunately, it is not understood.

A more concrete exposition of the same idea is the macrocosm-microcosm duality that was so popular in the art and philosophy of the Middle Ages. It may be useful to consider it as a way of getting at the Hermetic maxim.

The macrocosm was understood to be the universe that lay beyond the boundary of the human body and mind, all that was outside. The microcosm was the body itself and the mind and soul, all that lay encased in the envelope of flesh. The theory said in part that the body of man was a faithful replica in miniature of the greater body of the world. By studying the universe, many secrets could be learned about human nature; conversely by studying man, principles could be derived that would apply to the greater world. The magical side of it was the notion that actions committed in one "cosm" would affect the other. For example, that the position of the planets and stars influenced the qualities of men at their birth.

But the average thinker of the Middle Ages had a skewed perception when he considered the reasons underlying the correspondence of macrocosm and microcosm. In his view a third party, God, had created the world, and afterwards fashioned man to fit into the world, making him conformable with nature. This presupposition made true understanding impossible, because it diverted attention away from the underlying mechanism involved.

To grasp the Hermetic maxim, it is necessary to alter perception. There is no inside and outside. Inside and outside are oneside. The microcosm and macrocosm are not separate creations of God, but one seamless whole.

The mind creates all forms and qualities using the input of the senses. What the mind cannot contemplate, or the senses convey, can never be known in any way at all. Effectively, it does not exist.

It is of course possible to postulate a God view, where there exist forms and qualities not perceivable by the mind of man, but such things would be utterly beyond human reach, and so would have no being for man.

Once this truth is accepted, the Hermetic maxim becomes not only comprehensible but inevitable. What is above *must* be like what is below, because both are formed, and limited, by their passage through the lens of the human mind. There can never be anything outside that does not correspond to something inside. Above and below are one pattern. The human mind provides the connecting medium of all things. Nothing is really separate from anything else.

A second change in perception is necessary in order to get

insight into the way divination works. This involves *time*. Time is thought of as being composed of three distinct parts: past, present and future. According to prevalent assumption, we occupy the present. We can look back into the past by means of memory and records, both historical and natural, but we can never know anything about the future.

In one popular metaphor a man is seated on a furiously racing train with his back to the engine. He cannot get off, nor can he turn around. He can only sit and watch the landscape recede behind him.

The trouble with this model is that it is absurd. Past, present and future do not exist. The past is gone, the future has yet to be, and the present is an infinitely thin line between these two fictions.

Einstein said that time is what keeps everything from happening at once. He was not being facetious. Time is a device of the mind to control and regulate reality. It is a way of ordering the diversity of things so they can be separately considered. Adepts who have reached a transcendental awareness can in some measure abolish the fiction of time, suggesting its true nature.

Casket. Wood, 21.5 cm. in length. A rune calendar is carved into the side panel. The other symbols indicate special days.

—Reproduced by permission of Nordiska Museum, Sweden

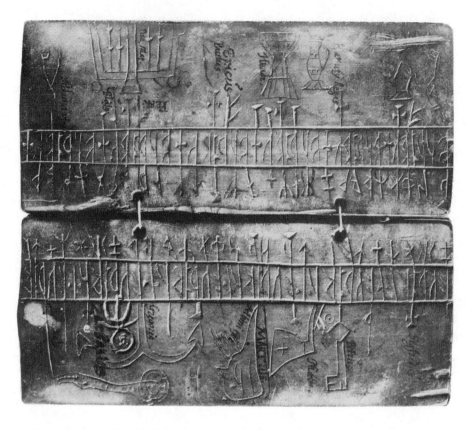

Rune Calendar. Wood. It is designed to fold together like a book to protect the runes.

—Reproduced by permission of Nordiska Museum, Sweden

Time is commonly thought of as analogous to a stream of spoken words. The words already perceived have ceased to be. The words to come are unknown to the listener. Only the actual fragment of the word vibrating on the lips exists, and how infinitely thin is that fragment!

Better to look upon time as a series of words printed in a book. The entire text of the book exists and is accessible to the reader, but cannot be apprehended all at once because the mind requires that the words be separated and differentiated. They lose their meaning when jumbled together. Yet the reader who speaks them aloud has access to any set of words, both before and after the point he or she is considering. Only the ignorant listener, who cannot see the book, is bound to the spoken words alone.

Time and space are both continuous, both conditional creations of the mind. Everything everywhere touches and mutually influences. It has truly been stated that there is no such thing as chance, only causes as yet unknown.

A life forms a zig-zagging diagonal track on the doughnut-shaped interlocking spiral skin of the universe; a line in time and space. At each point in that lifeline where a decision occurs, a node exists with two or more branching rays. Only one ray is the actual path traced by that life—the others are theoretical ghosts of tracks that would have been traced had other decisions been made.

Not for nothing did the ancient Teutons look upon the universe as a great ash. A tree begins from a single seed, branches into two, then four, then eight, soon becoming extremely intricate. The difference between a tree and a man is that all the branches on a tree are realized, whereas in human life only one continuous line exists; at least, in our dimension of consciousness.

The process of divination seeks to extend awareness into the future and trace that single line by relying on a correspondence between the greater world of man and the smaller world of the runes. Cut from the world tree, the runes accurately reflect its pattern; that is to say, because they germinated in the dark, rich soil of the unconscious, they can embody and convey its meanings.

Although divination is usually employed to look into the future, the runes can just as readily open a view on the past, or the present. This is useful if it becomes necessary to search into conditions that currently exist, but are hidden, in order to understand an ongoing circumstance. The past events in the life of an individual may provide needed information concerning his present nature. Time is continuous, all of one piece. Any area can be isolated and examined if the runes are rightly directed.

All the effort in divination is to present to the conscious mind what the unconscious mind already knows. The abundance of techniques is an effort extending over centuries to find the best instrument for bridging this self-created gulf. The runes are effective because they themselves were created, not by any one person, but by a race out of the primal stuff of the unconscious. Perhaps the only other instrument equally effective is the Tarot, which had an analogous birth.

In the unconscious, all the possible branches of a life exist in potential. The unconscious has direct access to the primal matrix from which emerges time and space. But for any separate moment considered, only one branch will extend as a necessary line of cause and effect. The unconscious can trace this line because it knows all causes and all effects. Chance is a meaningless word to omniscience.

There are two phases to divination: an inbreathing and an outbreathing.

The first is active. It is necessary to particularize from the infinite information in the unconscious mind the details desired—to locate the tiny twig that is of interest on the great tree of life. This is done by forming the question asked of the runes in the conscious mind and transferring it with desire by an act of Will into the runes, whichever rune instrument may be used.

The question must be very clearly conceived, and then made to pass out of the awareness and into the runes. This transference should be imagined physically, as a flow of essence, or force. Only if the question leaves the conscious mind can it enter the unconscious.

This is the cause of most failures in divination. The question is never asked rightly, and so no true answer can emerge. It is not possible to completely forget the question, since then the answer would have no meaning, but it is possible to release any desire or urgency about the question, to make it merely a neutral pattern of words and images, so that its essential vitality is transferred to the inner, hidden mind.

It requires a splitting of the mind well-known to all who

work in magic ritual. One part of the awareness is made detached and indifferent. The other part remains alert and watchful.

The second phase of divination is passive. The awareness must make itself receptive to impressions from the runes. Any attempt to force the runes into a preconceived pattern will end in failure. Moreover, the runes will react with hostility and begin to present mocking and malicious meanings, until they are completely useless for divination work.

Anyone who doubts this has only to make the experiment. Treat the counsel of the runes with contempt and you will receive contempt in return. The desire to read a favorable outcome must always be resisted. *Divination requires utter impartiality.* The proper attitude is one of reverence, which will yield the best results.

It is much easier to read the future of another person, because detachment is easier. But it is possible to achieve a state of detachment and tranquility regarding one's own future, if diligent efforts are made. This may sound like a contradiction in terms, but you must try not to try, and then success will come.

If the divination is viable, the runes will feel alive. They will seem to speak mutely to the understanding. Their shapes will embody specific meanings related directly to the question. In ancient times it was thought that the gods and goddesses spoke through them. There is a definite sense that they are being positioned and energized by an awareness other than that of the diviner.

It is necessary to actively follow the impressions that arise from the runes with the reason, weaving them together into a single whole. Meaning is built up from separate elements organically. One insight will lead to another:

> From a word to a word
> I was led to a word,
> from a deed to another deed.

At all times resist the temptation to put meanings into the runes. This will extinguish their fire and kill the reading.

Meaning is conveyed from the unconscious to the conscious mind, physically and psychically.

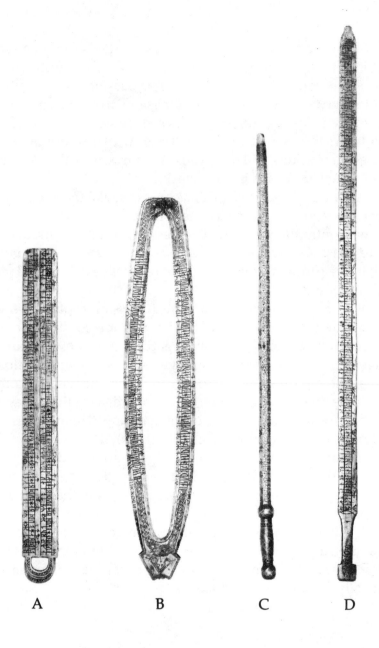

A   B   C   D

Rune Staves. A: Calendar staff, wood. B: Rune staff in a shape symbolic of the open womb. This same figure is often found in Christian art surrounding Christ. C and D: Rune staves in the shape of swords. A carryover from the days when runes were inscribed on military weapons for magical power.

—Reproduced by permission of Nordiska Museum, Sweden

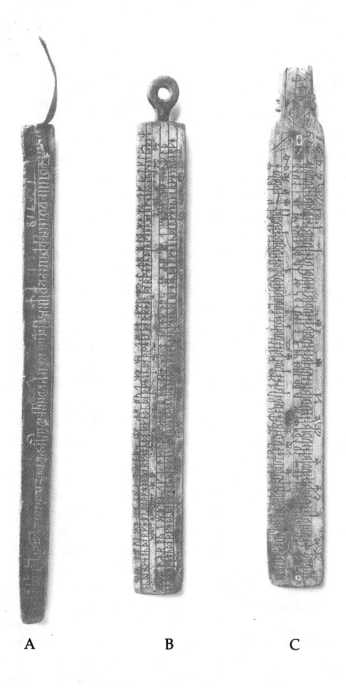

Rune staves. A: Wood. Approximately 60 cm. in length. B: Wood. Approximately 60 cm. in length. C: Calendar staff. Wood. Length: 62 cm.; width: 7 cm. The two rows of runes indicate days from January 1 to April 1, and from April 2 to July 1.

—Reproduced by permission of Nordiska Museum, Sweden

Physically, the fall of the runes depends on the muscular movements of the person who casts them. It would be impossible to influence their fall consciously without employing some material agency—in the same way that dice are influenced by weighting them with lead. Without such intervention, the vast number of contributing forces makes their fall random, as science understands the term. The conscious mind could never begin to coordinate even a tiny fraction of the force vectors involved.

It is another story with the unconscious, which has an infinite capacity. It can and does direct the fall of the runes via involuntary actions of the muscles. Although their fall appears uninfluenced, it is actually shaped to reveal the desired answer to the question asked.

Psychically, the pattern of the runes must be interpreted. Each rune is rich with associations. Only a fraction have been presented in this book. For every conceived meaning there are innumerable other associations that can only be intuited, or felt; never articulated.

From this limitless store of meaning, the awareness, directed by the unconscious, selects those elements that have bearing on the question. All other associations of the runes are temporarily veiled, so as not to distract the attention. This is why the story revealed by the runes can be so incredibly detailed and clear. There is an unperceived selection of specific meanings going on below the surface of the mind.

It would not be simplistic to regard that agency in the unconscious that responds through the runes as the rune gods. There is much practical value in such a convention. It provides names and forms, which can be manipulated, in place of amorphous forces, which cannot. Rune gods and goddesses can be appealed to, and if believed in, they will respond. A prayer to Odin, for example, before any rune divination, can increase the active energy of the runes. The efficacy of such a prayer will grow with repetition. The proof of this is left to experiment.

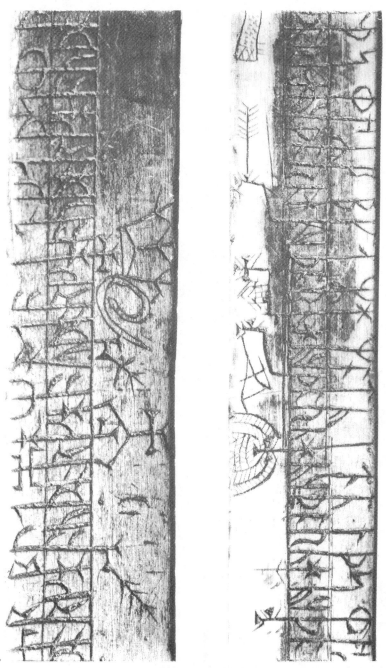

Rune staff. Wood, from 1592, from Uppland, a province on the eastern coast of Sweden.

Chapter 11

DIVINATION BY RUNES

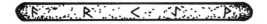

First Method: Rune Wands

Divination by rune wands is the traditional method. It is the most difficult and time consuming if done with the necessary care, but yields the best results. As nearly as possible, this first technique is a reconstruction of the ancient way of casting the runes, with its magical significance restored.

The period of preparation is nine days and nights. Render yourself ritually pure through moderate fasting, meditation and cleansing. Invoke the names of the greater Teutonic gods each morning and evening and pray that the coming divination will be successful. Contemplate the question each day passively without analyzing it in your mind. Avoid all excesses of drink, sleep, exercise, study, sex and other activities.

On the morning of the tenth day before the sun is above the horizon, go to the nearest wood and select a mature deciduous tree—one that bears fruit or nuts such as the apple, cherry, chestnut or oak. The oak qualifies because its acorns were used as mast for pigs. At the instant of sunrise, strike off a good sized branch with a previously purified and consecrated knife. The knife is purified by sprinkling it with water and exposing it to an open flame. It is consecrated by offering it in prayer to the service of the rune gods, particularly Odin. Try to sever the stem of the branch with a single blow. Using the same knife make a small cut in the palm of your right hand and apply a drop of blood to the stump of the limb on the tree.

The act of cutting the bough is done with sorrow in the heart at the injury committed against the tree. Your regret must be genuine; if you shed tears they may take the place of your blood on the stump. It is fitting to express your grief verbally in a prayer for the health and growth of the tree.

Carry the branch to the place of divination. An open space is best, but if inside it should be beneath a window where the light of the sky enters. Open the window if weather conditions permit. The ritual place should previously have been purified and consecrated. Sprinkle water in a circle and expose the area to the smoke and light of an open flame. With prayer and gestures, pledge the place to the glory of Odin.

Using the knife, cut the branch into 24 wands, each approximately nine inches in length. The wands must be thick enough to carve runes upon. Each wand receives one rune. Allow the shavings to fall on the open ground. If this is not possible, carefully gather them up and cast them over tranquil earth.

As you carve each rune, speak its name aloud and vibrate it inwardly. In effect this baptizes the runes and gives them their individual identity. When finished carving, recite a prayer that the wands may prove auspicious in their use. Stain the runes red. If the divination is of only moderate importance paint or powdered pigment may be used, but if the question has vital significance it is best to use your blood.

Blood feeds the runes. It is the most personal sacrifice that can be made. However, only the blood of the diviner is any good. The blood of another person or an animal is worse than useless because it costs you no pain or loss. Indeed, by using the blood of another being as a substitute for your own you merely emphasize your baseness before the gods, who value courage above all virtues.

The blood of the querent—a person who has come to you with a question—will not serve. Although the divination is performed for his or her benefit, it is the diviner who consults the runes, and the diviner who must pay the price.

When the stain is dry, spread a white cloth over the ground. It is best made of linen and should be at least four feet square. It may be ornamented at the edge or left a modest white. Above all it must be spotlessly clean, as it acts the part of a magic altar. Consecrate the cloth before the divination and never use it for a non-magical purpose. Purification should be unnecessary if the cloth is new.

Sit before the cloth on the ground or floor, and holding the rune wands over your heart next to your skin, speak the purpose of the divination. Ask that its auspices be true and that you be protected from all harm during the ritual on the authority of Odin, the All-Father. Closing your eyes, extend your hand over the cloth and draw an inward clockwise spiral with three revolutions in the air with the wands. Mentally draw energy down along the spiral. Open your hand forcefully so that the runes fly out and scatter over the cloth. With eyes shut pick up three runes at random.

The runes are read in order. The first refers to the past or the circumstances that gave rise to the question. The second rune gives the present on-going situation of the querent. The third indicates the course of future events and provides a comment on the outcome.

If two or more of the runes are favorable, the situation is not serious. If two or more runes are unfavorable, the potential for an outcome of harmful consequences exists. A hopeful rune at the end may indicate that conditions will improve.

Each rune belongs to one of the three *aettir*. Those under Feoh relate to material matters. They affect the stomach, bowels and lower body. Runes under the domain of Haegl relate to the emotional level. They affect the heart and lungs, and the arms. Runes under Tyr relate to the intellectual and spiritual part of the querent. They affect the head and organs of sense.

Of course all runes operate on all levels and can be either

good or bad depending on their circumstances. The division of the *aettir* is only a way of sorting out the various influences that must be considered. The context in which a rune is read always takes precedence over its *aett*.

The three runes Feoh, Haegl and Tyr are pivotal. When one occurs in a reading it indicates an abrupt change of attitude or situation. Haegl is a change for the worse, Feoh a change for the better, and Tyr a change of environment or personal elements that does not decide the matter under question.

When the divination is complete, destroy the runes by fire so they will not be profaned. You should have a small fire or charcoal brazier burning in the center of the ritual place. Never use runes that have been cut for a single specific purpose more than once. Watch the fire until the wands have been reduced to a fine ash, allow the ash to cool and then scatter it on the wind. Be careful that no glowing cinders remain in the ash that might set the woods on fire! It is best to cast the ash over a stream or pond where this is possible.

This form of rune wand divination will only be practiced on rare and great occasions due to its difficulty. Its physical elements alone consume the better part of a full day, to say nothing of the nine days of complex and tedious preparation. Many will not be wiling to draw their own blood or even to venture out of doors in the pre-dawn chillness. To them it can only be said that magic is not an easy discipline. It is a field that yields what is sown into it. Where there is no sacrifice there is no growth.

On more casual occasions, a set of rune wands that have been fashioned and retained may be used. Because these are not burned, they can be made more finely.

Select a board of new wood for its freedom from knots and straight grain. Oak or fruitwood should be chosen. Cut the board into 24 strips nine inches long, one inch wide, and about one-eighth inch thick. Taper the ends. Sand the wands to uniform size and thickness. Cut one rune into each wand across the grain, leaving the back of the wand blank. Fill the runes with scarlet paint using a fine artist's brush. Polish them with hard wax.

Once the wands are made they must be consecrated. Indicate in your ritual that the wands will be used repeatedly. Frequent proper use will increase their power. It is not necessary to shed blood in the making of these wands, although it often happens that a tool will slip, and a few drops of blood will fall. If this occurs, touch the blood to each wand.

Traditionally carpenters believed no important piece of furniture could be made rightly without the accidental shedding of blood. They welcomed it, and pressed their blood into their work. If blood was not shed it was considered unlucky. The magical overtones of this practice will at once be obvious. It may even be a direct descendant of rune magic.

The wands can be wrapped in white linen to preserve them from profane sight or touch, but it is better to fashion a box of clear pine. Pine is the most often used wood for storing magical instruments because of its neutral and benign associations. The explanation usually given is that pine is opaque to astral influences.

These finished wands can be employed in the same way described above, but without the nine days' preparation. Some mental preparation is desirable if the divination is to have any degree of success. If treated with proper reverence, the wands will give good results, particularly after long use.

Another technique of divination that can be applied to the rough or smooth wands is to let them fall upon the white cloth with the usual preparations and prayers, but instead of picking up three wands separately, they are read as a group according to the way they have fallen.

Some basic guidelines must be followed to make sense out of the pattern. The wands are read in order according to their distance away from the diviner. Wands of equal distance are considered together. Read only those wands that have landed face up; do not disturb the pattern or turn any wands over.

Crossed wands indicate opposing influences. Wands that touch are directly related. Wands lying parallel are in harmony or accord, and support each other. A wand between two others is divided in its influence. One wand on top of another dominates it. Wands facing downward do not count, however, and should be ignored. If many upright wands are piled across a single wand, its power will be suppressed or hidden.

Consideration should be given to the overall appearance of the pattern. If it is ordered and geometric, the outcome will also be orderly. If it is chaotic, with the appearance of an explosion or windstorm, the outcome will be stormy. When most of the runes fall face up, the question will be readily revealed and all things made plain in short order. When most runes fall face down, the matter of the divination is obscure and hidden, and likely to remain so. Should all runes fall face down, no further inquiry should be made.

If the rune wands are widely spread away from you, the time span for the working out of the matter will be long. If they are bunched together, a resolution will occur quickly. A gap between two groups of wands points to a span of time during which nothing much will occur. This must be patiently waited out.

Individual runes are read as before, according to their associations and their *aett*.

This pattern technique yields very complete and detailed readings into difficult questions, especially those that cover a major portion of a life. It is recommended where subtle shades of meaning are required.

Second Method: Rune Cards

Cut 24 rectangles of thin, stiff cardboard of a size that can conveniently be held in the hand. On one side of each card paint with flat red paint one of the runes. Lines should be made with a single stroke of the brush moving to the right and downward. The runes fill the face of the cards. The effect will be similar to Japanese calligraphy if the runes are executed with firm, bold brush strokes.

Additional information such as the name of the rune, its short meaning, its transliteration, its *aett*, may be added in black ink at the corners. A decorative design may be put on the backs—this should be kept simple since it will have to be reproduced for each card. When all the desired information is complete, coat the cards with clear satin varnish and stand them up to dry. Use a solvent-based varnish, not one of the new water-based, as the latter will make the ink run.

The cards must be purified and consecrated before use. The gods of Teutonic myth should be included in the consecration ceremony, with Odin as the central figure. It is best to do purification and consecration on separate days, making each act a solemn ritual. However, if necessary they can be combined. Once consecrated the cards are holy instruments and must be treated with reverence. Keep them apart, away from the sight or touch of others, in a pine box or linen wrap.

Rune cards are used in much the same way as the Tarot. The querent holds the cards for a moment and focuses his or her will on them with a question in mind. It is better if the diviner also knows the question. The diviner shuffles the cards thoroughly and cuts them, then deals out three in a row left to right. Each card is turned top to bottom as it is read, beginning with the left card and moving across to the right.

If finer shades of meaning are desired, the cards that are upside down after they are turned over can be read with a negative interpretation. This is left to the discretion of the diviner, but it must be decided upon before the reading begins. Remember that the cards are inverted when they are turned. They should be read according to their attitude after turning.

Cards are read in the same manner as rune wands. The card on the left represents the past, the card in the middle the present, and the card on the right the future. A good final card is a sign that the situation will improve. The three runes that name the *aettir* are of special significance and dominate the reading when they appear.

Another slightly more involved spread, or pattern for laying out the cards, is one called the *Five Elements Spread*. The rune deck is shuffled and cut, then four cards are laid out in a square cross, first the vertical arm from top to bottom, then the horizontal arm from left to right. In the center is placed a fifth card:

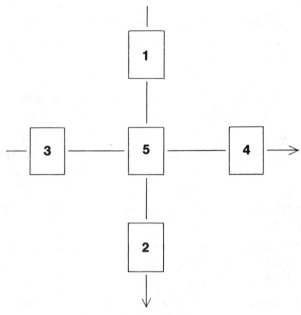

Five Elements Spread

The spread represents the macrocosm of the world and the microcosm of the human body. The vertical arm is the axis of the Earth and the human spinal column. The horizontal arm is a circle seen edgewise that surrounds the vertical axis: the equator of the Earth and the senses of the body. The fifth card is the center of creation, the fountain of life, the human heart. The cross is viewed from the back and can be fitted to the human body standing facing the South.

The *first* card at the top of the vertical arm is the intellect. It is masculine and relates to studies, invention, composition, mathematics, science, and the classical arts. In Teutonic mythology the god closest in nature to this point is Tiw, god of judgment. The card marks the North and the philosophical element Air, which is related to thought. Its instrument is the Sword; its archangel Raphael; its figure the Angel. It touches the forehead in man.

The *second* card at the bottom of the vertical arm is desire. It is masculine and relates to battles, lust, cruelty, anger, hatred and works of destruction. In Teutonic mythology the god most like this point is Thor. The card marks the South and the element

Fire, which is violent emotion. Its instrument is the Rod; its archangel Michael; its figure the Lion. It touches the sex in man.

The *third* card at the left end of the horizontal arm is strength. It is feminine and relates to labor, endurance, persistence, silence, suffering and woe. In Teutonic myth this point is similar to the goddess Nerthus. The card marks the East and the element Earth, which is mute striving and travail. Its instrument is the Disk; its archangel Uriel; its figure the Bull. It touches the left hand of severity in man.

The *fourth* card at the right end of the horizontal arm is love. It is feminine and relates to family, friendships, devotion, obsession, illusions, fantasy and the lyrical arts. In Teutonic myth the goddess Frija is most like this point. The card marks the West and the element Water, which is glamour. Its instrument is the Cup; its archangel Gabriel; its figure the Eagle. It touches the right hand of mercy in man.

The *fifth* card at the center is associated with balance. From it the four elements are born and to it they return. It represents the querent. It is sexually androgynous and relates to politics, religion and magic. Its keynote is responsibility. In Teutonic myth a god very similar in nature to the center point is Balder. The card marks the center of being and the element Light, which is cosmos. Its instrument is the Lamp; its archangel Christ; its figure Man. It touches the heart of man.

With this spread a detailed analysis of the life and character of a person can be obtained. It is used where depth of understanding into the personality is required, and is excellent as a follow-up inquiry after the first simple three card spread.

Another pattern for laying out the cards is called the *Seven Planets Spread.* Six cards are dealt face down on the points of an imaginary hexagram, and a seventh card is placed in the center. First the upward-pointing triangle of the hexagram is laid out clockwise, beginning at the topmost point; then the downward-pointing triangle is laid out, also clockwise, beginning at the lowermost point. The central card is placed last:

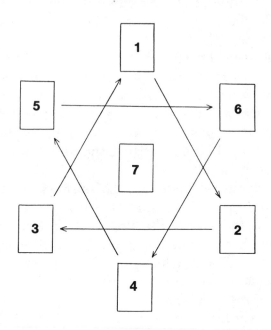

Seven Planets Spread

The cards are turned and read in the same order they were laid out.

The *first* card relates to the Sun and its qualities of warmth, health, light, strength, happiness, and pleasure. It stands for the father, or a mature man with wealth.

The *second* card relates to Mars and its qualities of courage, boldness, sexual potency, battle, strife, conflict, and trial. It stands for the brother, or a young man of action.

The *third* card relates to Saturn and its qualities of gravity, physical strength, endurance, coldness, dullness, age, and material things. It stands for an elderly relative who may be male or female, or an old person in the church, law or business.

The *fourth* card relates to the Moon and its qualities of beauty, mystery, magic, illusion, fascination, glamour, secrets, illness and madness. It stands for the mother, or a mature woman in the arts.

The *fifth* card relates to Venus and its qualities of love, affection, desire, lust, pleasure, adornment, display, and fertility. It stands for the sister, or a young beautiful woman of an amorous nature.

The *sixth* card relates to Jupiter and its qualities of command, order, dominance, rule, authority, government, joviality, prosperity, wealth and leadership. It stands for an older male relative in good health, or an older man in a position of authority.

The *seventh* card relates to Mercury and its qualities of intelligence, adaptability, learning, skill, artistry, responsiveness, balance, and magical knowledge. It stands for the querent.

The cards that form the upward triangle of the hexagram are predominantly masculine in their influence—active, direct, open, forceful. The cards that form the downward triangle are mostly feminine in their effect—hidden, indirect, passive, diffuse. The central card stands for the querent and gives the keynote to the reading.

If it is useful to break the spread into time units, cards one, two and three suggest the past—what is already known. Cards four, five and six relate to the future—what is still hidden. Card seven points to the present.

Runes that fall on opposite points of the hexagram are likely to be of opposing influence. Runes on the same triangle will be harmonious and reinforce each other. The central rune balances the others.

Many Tarot spreads work well with rune cards. As a rule simple spreads work better than complex spreads. There is really no need to use an involved process for selecting the cards or a maze-like pattern in laying them out. If the runes wish to speak they will do so—simplicity will not obstruct them. If you are inwardly prepared, any spread will work; if you are not ready in your heart, complexities will only distract and fatigue the mind.

Third Method: Rune Dice
Cut four one-inch cubes from some fruitwood. Oak is good because of its magical associations and attractive grain. After

sanding and polishing them to uniform size, clamp them in a vise and cut one rune in each of the 24 facets. Pairs of runes should be placed on opposite faces of the same cube:

1st cube	2nd cube	3rd cube	4th cube

Paint the grooves of the runes red. Finish the dice with hard wax, taking care not to pack the runes with wax. Purify and consecrate the dice and store them in a pouch of linen or a small box of pine.

When conducting a divination, give the dice to the querent for a moment to blow on. This act is the equivalent to shuffling the cards and allows the querent a personal physical involvement in the divination. If you are divining for yourself, blow on the dice. After a brief prayer and a moment of concentration on the question, cast the dice over a consecrated white cloth.

The runes that fall uppermost are recorded on a piece of paper in order based on their distance from you—the nearest rune is written first on the left. The dice are cast twice more and the runes written down above the first set:

3rd cast	9	10	11	12	Future
2nd cast	5	6	7	8	Present
1st cast	1	2	3	4	Past

The first cast of the dice represents the past circumstances of the question or some important event or trait in the life of the querent. The second cast stands for the present situation and reveals what may be hidden but is currently impinging on the question. The third cast is the future of the matter and its outcome.

Special attention should be given to the first and last runes. The first suggests the general tone of the matter. The last gives a prognostication of whether it will end well or ill. If one of the runes signifying the three *aettir* (Feoh, Haegl or Tyr) occurs in a line, that line should be read within the context of that *aett*. Feoh is physical and mild. Haegl is emotional and severe. Tyr is mental and balanced.

Those with a knowledge of astrology can read the runes in relation to the twelve houses of the Zodiac. Briefly, the influence of each house is:

First House	Beginnings. Childhood. Physical and mental characteristics.
Second House	Money matters. Business. Possessions.
Third House	Relationships and relations. Acquaintances. Neighbors. Communications.
Fourth House	The home. Parents. Ancestors. Inheritances. Skeletons in the closet. Endings.
Fifth House	Loves and affections. Rewards and satisfactions. Children. Gambling.
Sixth House	Health. Work. Service. Hygiene. Mental state. Also servants and employees.
Seventh House	Marriage and law. Partnerships. Contracts. Divorces. Disagreements.
Eighth House	Sexual matters. Death and related legacies and insurance. The Occult.
Ninth House	Religion. Visions. Dreams. Philosophy. Journeys. Studies.
Tenth House	Career. Fame. Promotion. Politics. Ambitions.

Eleventh House   Friends and acquaintances. Groups and clubs. Hopes and aspirations.

Twelfth House   Limitations. Restrictions. Confinement. Secrets. Sacrifice. The unconscious.

A simpler way of using the dice is to cast them once and read them as they fall according to their meaning and pattern. The nearest die is read first and stands for the past, or background. The two middle dice represent the present, or ongoing circumstance. The die that lands farthest away shows the future, or outcome.

Two dice together have complementary meanings. If they touch, their effects will be united and occur almost simultaneously. If a die lands tipped at an angle against something, its rune is uncertain or changeable. Consider both runes that show on its upper facets, giving more weight to the one most exposed. Should a die roll very far away, the outcome of the matter will be delayed for a considerable time. The closer together the dice fall, the shorter the time span required to determine the question.

This technique is useful when a very quick reading is desired into a simple and relatively trivial matter.

For purposes of divination, the runes must be applied to the practical day-to-day affairs of common life. The meanings given to them are more specific and restricted than the broader esoteric attributions of the runes considered as a whole. Here is a brief summary of the divinatory meanings for easy reference:

ᚠ   wealth, possession, ownership, dominion, opulence, luxury; but also cowardice, stupidity, dullness, slavery, bondage. A valuable object.

ᚢ   masculine potency, freedom, energy, action, courage, strength; but also lust, brutality, rashness, callousness, violence. Sexual desire.

ᚦ   evil, malice, hatred, torment, spite, lies; but also catharsis, nemesis, purging, cleansing fire. Signifies a bad man or woman.

ᚠ good, love, health, harmony, truth, wisdom, a revealing message or insight; but also vanity and grandiloquence. Signifies a good man or woman.

ᚱ travel, vacation, relocation, evolution, change of place or setting, may refer to transportation by car, ship or plane; but also disruption, dislocation; demotion, delusion, possibly a death. A journey.

ᚲ vision, revelation, knowledge, light, guidance, clarity; but also nakedness, exposure, loss of illusion and false hope. A beacon.

ᚷ gift, award, bequest, inheritance, legacy, offering; but also sacrifice, obligation, toll, privation. A present.

ᚹ joy, ecstasy, delight, glory, spiritual reward; but also delirium, intoxication, possession by higher forces, impractical enthusiasm. Happiness.

ᚻ pain, loss, suffering, hardship, sickness, affliction, natural disaster; but also tempering, testing, trial. Wrath of Nature.

ᚾ necessity, extremity, want, deprivation, starvation, need, poverty, emotional hunger; but also endurance, survival, determination, resistance. Defiance of circumstance.

ᛁ treachery, illusion, deceit, betrayal, guile, stealth, ambush, plots; but also glamour, allure, seduction, invitation, entrapment. A cunning and beautiful woman.

ᛟ alteration, transformation, turning, revolution of circumstance, fulfillment of plans; but also inversion, sudden setback, reversals. A major change.

ᛃ strength, reliability, dependability, trustworthiness; but also stolidness, lack of imagination or initiative. An honest man who can be relied upon.

ᛈ abundance, luxury, opulence, display, lavishness; but also debauchery, decadence, excess, superficiality, drunkenness, lasciviousness, gluttony. Physical pleasure.

ᛉ protection, defense, warding off of evil, shield, guardian; but also taboo, warning, turning away, that which repels. Signifies danger.

ᛊ power, elemental force, sword of flame, cleansing fire; but also destruction, retribution, justice, casting down of vanity. Wrath of God.

ᛏ victory, valor, battle prowess, discernment, winning of disputes and legal judgments; but also strife, war, conflict. A battle.

ᛒ growth, fertility, love, healing, arousal of desire; but also passion, carelessness, abandon, loss of control. A love affair or new birth.

ᛖ transportation, speed, movement, conveyance—may represent a horse, car, boat, plane, or other vehicle; but also blind precipitation, rushing in, reckless haste. Rapid progress.

ᛗ intelligence, forethought, craft, skill, ability; but also cunning, slyness, manipulation, craftiness, calculation. The magician.

ᛚ water, lake, river, ocean, dreams, fantasies, mysteries, the unknown, the hidden, the deep, the underworld; but also madness, obsession, despair, perversity, sickness, suicide. The unconscious.

ᛜ common virtues, common sense, simple strengths, family love, caring, human warmth; but also production, toil, labor, work, career. The home.

ᛞ a cycle, period, phase, span of a life, unit of time; but also ending, limit, coming full circle. A completion.

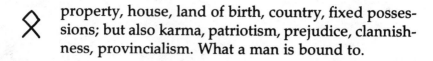 property, house, land of birth, country, fixed posses-
sions; but also karma, patriotism, prejudice, clannish-
ness, provincialism. What a man is bound to.

Chapter 12

CHANGE RUNES

The advantage in knowing the future is the power to control it. If all futures were rosy there would be no point in divination. Its value lies in revealing hurtful influences before they mature, or providing reassurance that a present circumstance will not evolve into something destructive. In either case it directs necessary action—what must, or need not, be done.

To change the future it is necessary to shift from one branch on the world ash Yggdrasill to another using the nodes formed by moments of decision. Each life follows one continuous tributary. Wherever a choice is possible, there exists a node, or juncture. When a choice is made, one pathway opens while the others are blocked. Divination projects a line into the future based on cause and effect: what will happen due to outer circumstances and inner nature.

It is not so easy to alter the prediction of the runes. True divination takes into account all factors that influence the question. There is no place for chance. It even considers its own influence. Therefore, a man reacting against the future he has divined may, by his actions, help to bring it to pass. Unwittingly he becomes part of its fulfillment.

To change the outcome of the runes he must step outside the matrix of the unconscious from which their verdict was drawn. As long as he stays within that closed circle, he can never alter the future, because he remains part of its cause and effect. In Eastern mystical terms, he is a prisoner of karma.

Only an act of free will can break the chain of cause and effect revealed by the runes. Free will is transcendent. It is born in the Unmanifest, and is not a part of the underlying fabric of the universe. Because it is outside the ring of karma, the runes are unable to take account of it in predicting the future. It is the true *deus ex machina* of life.

The most necessary thing to bring about an act of free will is to realize its absence in everyday existence. Most people have no awareness of their bondage, and so can never be anything other than slaves. They are automatons pushed and pulled about in the depths of a great machine; sleepers dancing in slow harmony to a single strain of music they cannot consciously hear.

However, acts of free will do occur in ordinary lives. Almost everyone transcends cause and effect at least on a few rare occasions, usually at moments of extreme stress. A decision that is free can be recognized by the sense of inevitability and power it carries with it. You can actually feel freedom; it has a unique quality. There is a calmness, even love, that is unmistakable once it has been experienced. In those moments when you feel anger and violence within, yet act with love; or those times you are oppressed by inertia and indifference, yet involve yourself, you may become free.

To change the future it is first necessary to understand the verdict of the runes in relation to the question, and to trace the chain of cause and effect with full awareness of its mechanical aspect. Then you must meditate sincerely and consider what outcome would not be a blind reaction to circumstance. Seek to imagine a future scenario that is healthful and positive. It must be absolutely free of hostility, envy, and all other negative feelings.

It is not necessary to consider what steps are required to achieve this scenario, only to conceive it with crystal clarity fulfilled and existent. Magic finds its own course to the sea. If you begin to speculate on ways to achieve your ideal state, your desire will hinder its occurrence. You must be prepared to follow the pathway your magic opens before you. It is futile to try to plot the path ahead of time—at best an intellectual exercise, at worst an obstruction.

You should, however, be aware that the free act necessary to change your future will occur at one of the nodes on your lifeline, a moment of decision where multiple branches diverge. It is not a good idea to try to create a node; that is, to force a decision. Again, this will generate desire which is part of cause and effect. Better to wait for a node to be reached, then when it feels right, to act according to intuition. Your act of true will is channeled by the magical preparation that will be described a little farther on.

There are two types of blind reaction to guard against. The first is passive. If you allow yourself to be moved by influences other than your heart of Self, even those that seem benign or useful, you are no more than a billiard ball knocked about the table by other equally enslaved balls. Such passive acceptance is everywhere in common life. The herd instinct, peer pressure, fashion, fads, cults, patriotism, mob violence, prejudice, are all different aspects of passive reaction.

The second type of reaction is active. Returning anger for anger, violence for violence, hate for hate, and even love for love on an elementary level, are examples of active reaction. For example, if a car cuts you off in traffic, and you in turn cut off some other car attempting to merge ahead of you, this is active reaction.

It is not necessarily more free to react against intimidation than acquiesce to it. Both are equally animal responses when the impulse does not originate with the true Will, which is the agent of the Higher Self. One may be more satisfying than the other, and here lies the danger—because it yields a momentary burst of satisfaction it is liable to be mistaken for a thing of value, which it is not. All reaction is valueless to the evolution of the soul. And more to the point in the present inquiry, no reaction will alter the future revealed by the runes.

Of course, it is here assumed that the divination has been properly executed and interpreted. If either was done wrongly it would require an act of free will to *fulfill* the prognostication!

The runes themselves give guidance on how to change the outcome of the reading. In any divination that cannot be accepted there are unfavorable elements, embodied in individual runes. The forces that these negative elements represent must first be analyzed and understood. Then counter-forces, in the form of runes with opposite potentials, can be applied to lessen or abolish their hurtful influence.

It may be easier to grasp the technique through a hypothetical example.

A woman needs to know if a man is seriously interested in her. She has been dating this man for some time. At first he was responsive and loving, but lately he has begun to show signs of coldness. She casts the rune wands, and draws up three in this order, from left to right:

The first rune, Sigel, stands for the active fire of the Sun and its potent energies. The position indicates that it applies to the past, and to influences on the question that underlie or define its circumstances. With regard to the relationship and the male lover, it tells of a fiery and active beginning, aggression, confidence—perhaps too much confidence. The sun bolt can easily become destructive.

The second rune, Lagu, stands for water, dreams, illusion, emotion, perhaps a wavering or uncertainty. The position indicates that it should be applied to the present, and to the heart of the subject under inquiry; in this case, the lover himself. The water rune directly applied to a male suggests contradiction, inner conflict, and weakness of an emotional nature.

The third rune, Feoh, stands for possessions of a moveable kind, ownership in general, and in a negative interpretation dullness, servitude and captivity. The position indicates that it applies to the future, the outcome of the question, and to influences that are developing and ripening.

Any set of runes can be interpreted in many different ways. Only one of these interpretations will be accurate. It is always necessary to allow intuition to act in revealing the runes. If the mind is open and impartial, one thread of meaning will rise above the others.

In this case, the woman remembers that at the start of the relationship she was cool and somewhat indifferent to the advances of the man because she did not then know if she cared for him. But as her love grew stronger, she became more demonstrative and active in pursuing his interest. She phoned him at his place of work, called unannounced at his apartment, and generally tried to make plain her affection. It was at this point that his passion cooled.

The interpretation lies in the third rune. The man fears that he is being aggressively led into a position from which he cannot escape. He feels himself manipulated, whether rightly or wrongly, and his unusually potent ego is threatened. This makes him uncertain how to respond, and he withdraws.

Understanding the present situation, and its prospects in the future, the woman must now decide what steps will counter the negative forces involved. She can choose to change the behavior of her lover, change the environment in which the affair exists, or change her own behavior.

The temptation is to put pressure on the man to impel him back into the relationship—either by arousing so strong a desire in him that it overcomes his qualms, or by altering material circumstances in his life so that he is thrown by social forces into her arms: creation of a mutual dependency or common financial interest, for example.

Upon reflection the woman realizes that these courses

would only extend the behavior on her part that alienated her lover in the first place. Also, she has no wish to change his basic nature since she is attracted to him as he is.

The alternative is to alter her own behavior in such a way that she is no longer producing an effect opposite to the one she desires. By being too demonstrative in trying to draw her lover to her, she has frightened him away. She must set the runes to act on herself internally so that she feels less anxiety over losing the man, and less urge to capture and possess him, since these are the emotions that have poisoned the affair.

Notice that it is not necessary for her to compromise her feelings or her ideals, only to control those involuntary reactions that are interfering with her happiness. At the same time she will invoke a healthful and balanced emotional atmosphere that will convey the changes she has undertaken to the attention of her lover. It is not necessary that he be consciously aware of any change in her, so long as it infiltrates his unconscious awareness.

Runes that are used to bring about personal transformation are called change runes. The woman chooses three of these to embody the forces she wants to bear on the relationship—three to balance the three runes of the divination. These are, from left to right:

The first of these, Eoh, reacts on the Sigel rune of the divination. The influence of Eoh is strength, reliance, continuity, endurance, fidelity, and related qualities. These do not counter the influence of Sigel, but add to it and enhance the forces that underlie the love relationship. Its fire is moderated and made steadier so it will burn longer.

The second rune, Man, reacts on Lagu in the divination. The influence of Man is awareness, capability, assurance, and clarity of purpose. It acts to dispel through insight and reason the confusion and emotional instability of the Lagu rune, applying to the central nature of the lover himself and allowing him to see the true motive of the woman.

The third rune, Ing, reacts on the Feoh rune of the divination. The influence of Ing is that of home and hearth; it carries associations of family, trust, selfless affection and honor. These lend to the passive qualities of Feoh a positive aspect, and the message of love through coercion becomes one of love through respect.

To activate these change runes requires the construction of a personal ritual based on the general ritual method given in Chapter 5, and the rune magic techniques of Chapter 6. The runes must be carved into, or bound to, some material or object that represents the focus of their desired effect—in the hypothetical case given above, the behavior of the woman herself and the way her lover perceives it.

The object may be a letter, a photograph, a piece of furniture, a gift, an article of clothing, but it is important that it have the most complete and precise association possible. In the example, a photograph of the woman and man taken together would serve to represent her behavior, his perception and the love relationship.

Each change rune must be considered specifically with regard to that portion of the divination it applies to, in order to focus its power. If not focused and directed that energy will be lost. It is not necessary to numerically reflect the divination. More or less runes may be used, perhaps only a single rune, but there must be a willed application of the change runes to the question.

To carry the example further, the woman chooses a photograph that shows both she and her lover together in happier times. She prepares herself mentally with prayer and ritual washing, goes to the place of ritual and invokes the patronage and favor of the god of love, Balder. Drawing the change runes on the back of the photograph with red ink, she wills them into the essence of the picture, visualizing her ideal manner, and the ideal reaction of her lover to her. She kisses each of the change runes reverently to empower them with love.

This ritual she repeats every day, and she waits and remains watchful for the coming of the node of decision that will enable her to actualize her purpose. She trusts to her intuition and the action of the change runes, that she will recognize the moment and act rightly when it arrives. The repetition of the ritual builds a kind of magical charge that arcs across the node.

It is best to retain the change runes between repetitions of the change ritual, rather than to attempt to send them on one of the elements. That way the potent associations of the object to which they are affixed will not be lost. The runes will continue to work on the object, and by magical sympathy, the problem, between their ritual charging.

Whatever the form of the ritual that is devised, it must be repeated often and regularly. Beginners in magic sometimes think a ritual will be effective the first time it is conducted. This occasionally occurs. More generally, results are built up over time through repetition. Many, many repetitions may be needed before the runes begin to blaze with their own fire and come truly alive. A well-known maxim in magic is: "Invoke Often."

It is, however, not so necessary to believe in the efficacy of ritual as is generally thought. When it is worked with an open mind, accurate procedure, and repetition, results will follow, as surely as day follows night. To some extent magic is an automatic process. In the same way that muscles must be built up through proper exercise, magical effects must follow properly executed rituals. It takes a perverse ingenuity to perform a ritual correctly and often, yet get no results at all.

When they are not in actual use, store the change runes, and the object they are written upon, out of sight in clean white linen, or blue silk. Let no other person see or touch them, unless you have assistants in the ritual. At all costs do not talk about them, and if others ask what you are doing, remain silent.

Whatever the structure of the personal change ritual you devise, in it you will be focusing upon the change runes and charging them with power through your will, then channeling that power into the object representing the question of the previous divination, the outcome of which you wish to alter.

Picture in your mind the change runes working to shift the life-stem from one branch of Yggdrasill to another. Imagine as concretely as possible the effect you wish to bring about occurring through the action of the runes, and conveyed through the association of the object on which they are carved or written. Do *not* imagine the original runes of the divination, or picture the situation they predicted. Make no effort to avoid these thoughts, as this will surely bring them about. Rather, concentrate solely on the change runes and their effect.

If the ritual is conducted often, as will usually be necessary, it may not be desirable to feed the runes with blood each time. Blood will strengthen the working of the runes, but if there is a reluctance to draw it day after day, any useful effect will be negated by that unconscious resistance. To be a sacrifice, blood must be given freely. The problem may not arise in change rituals that involve other fluids of the body, which are more readily obtained.

The appropriate gods should be invoked to oversee the operation of the change ritual. Remember the gods are living spirits with personalities that must be dealt with and appealed to, if the desired results are to follow. Never make the mistake of looking upon the gods as metaphors for psychological forces. This is fatal. The gods are real, and you had best regard them as real if you want them to act in your behalf.

For works of love, invoke Freyja or Frey. For strictly physical desire, Frija; but for spiritual love, Balder. For works of obligation, duty, office, or honor, invoke Tiw. For works of war, discord, strife, or physical trial, invoke Thor. For any work regarding magic, artistry, craftsmanship, or skill, invoke Odin. For works of deceit, deception, confusion, division, or malice, invoke Loki—but watch it! For works of patience, endurance, and constancy, invoke Heimdall. For necromancy, invoke Hel.

These categories apply to all rune magic, not merely when using change runes to alter the future.

Call the gods through their associations (colors, metals,

personal objects, and so on) and by visualizing their forms. Placate them by showing an awareness of their function and nature, their role in the scheme of things. Activate them through prayer and ritual enactment.

Prayer to a rune god should take the form of a statement of purpose and an expression of thanks. Honor the gods with appropriate words. This is a kind of sacrifice—a sacrifice of the mind, called "reasonable sacrifice"—which will feed the gods and empower them to act in your behalf. Reasonable sacrifice to the Highest, who is Nameless and Formless, is silence. All lesser gods are honored through their attributes.

Never humble yourself before the rune god, or grovel, or beg. These actions serve no function. Never promise a gift to a rune god for services rendered. If the service is given, a payment will surely be exacted. It is not for you to determine in advance what it should be, or to try to reduce or limit it.

Invoking the appropriate god during the change ritual will give greater force to the change runes. The god will serve as an agent in employing them. Of course the appropriate god will act in any case, even if it is not called by name, but calling him or her increases the ease of the god's intervention.

As stated before, the key to changing the future lies not in the technique, but in knowing what should, and should not, be changed. Everyone has heard stories about people who learn their fate and try to avoid it, but through their frantic efforts only succeed in bringing about the doom they sought to shun. Such fiction has a moral in it for rune magicians. Change the future if you must, but think before you act.

APPENDIX I

Rune Gods/Goddesses — Associations

Deities	Color	Metal	Object	Rune*	Firewood	Jewel
Balder	yellow	gold	bow	ᛞ	mistletoe	topaz
Heimdall	blue	steel	horn	ᛋ	yew	sapphire
Loki	mist grey	arsenic	shoes	ᚦ	thorn	opal
Thor	orange	tin	hammer	ᛋ	oak	jasper
Tiw	red	iron	sword	↑	fir	ruby
Odin	white	mercury	spear	ᚱ	ash	diamond
Frija	green	copper	necklace	ᛕ	apple	emerald
Hel	black	lead	veil	ᛁ	willow	jet
Freyja	purple	silver	cloak	ᛒ	birch	amethyst
Frey	red-brown	bronze	chariot	ᛦ	pine	tree agate

* The runes are those that most closely approximate the qualities of the gods. They should not be confused with the runes used in Chapter 7, which stand for elemental qualities.

RUNE ALPHABETS

	Germanic		Old English		Old Norse		Gothic
�492	fehu	ᚠ	feoh	ᚠ	fehu	ᚠ	faihu
ᚢ	uruz	ᚢ	ur	ᚢ	uruR	ᚢ	urus
ᚦ	thurisaz	ᚦ	thorn	ᚦ	thurisaR	ᚦ	thuris
ᚨ	ansuz	ᚫ	os	ᚯ	ansuR	ᚯ	ansus
ᚱ	raido	ᚱ	rad	ᚱ	raidu	ᚱ	raida
ᚲ	kenaz	ᚺ	cen	ᚤ	kauna	ᚲ	kusma
ᚷ	gebo	ᚷ	gyfu			ᚷ	giba
ᚹ	wunjo	ᚹ	wyn			ᚹ	winja
ᚾ	hagalaz	ᚾ	haegl	ᚼ	hagla	ᚾ	hagl
ᛏ	nauthiz	ᛏ	nyd	ᚼ	naudiR	ᛏ	nauths
ᛁ	isa	ᛁ	is	ᛁ	isaR	ᛁ	eis
ᛃ	jera	ᛇ	ger	ᛃ	jara	ᛆ	jer
ᛇ	eihwaz	ᛇ	eoh			ᛇ	aihus
ᛈ	perth	ᛈ	peord			ᛈ	pairthra
ᛉ	algiz	ᛉ	eolh	ᛦ	algiR	ᛉ	algs
ᛋ	sowelu	ᛋ	sigel	ᚿ	sowelu	ᛋ	sauil
ᛏ	teiwaz	ᛏ	tir	ᛏ	tiwaR	ᛏ	teiws
ᛒ	berkana	ᛒ	beorc	ᛒ	berkana	ᛒ	bairkan
ᛖ	ehwaz	ᛖ	eh			ᛖ	egeis
ᛗ	mannaz	ᛗ	man	ᛦ	mannaR	ᛗ	manna
ᛚ	laguz	ᛚ	lagu	ᛚ	laguR	ᛚ	lagus
ᛜ	inguz	ᛜ	ing			ᛜ	iggws
ᛟ	othila	ᛟ	ethel			ᛟ	othal
ᛞ	dagaz	ᛞ	daeg			ᛞ	dags
		ᚪ	ac				
		ᚫ	aesc				

othila ⎱ inver.
dagaz ⎰

Germanic	Old English	Old Norse	Gothic
	ᛙ yr		
	ᛠ ear		
	ᛡ ior		
	ᛣ calc		
	ᚸ gar		
	ᛢ cweord		
	ᛥ stan		

The names of the runes have been modernized and Anglicized (some might say bastardized) to spare the reader the thicket of phonetic symbols that would otherwise infest them. Students of ancient languages will find these versions deplorable, but it is hoped all others will find them workable compromises.

Germanic runes **Anglo Saxon additions** **Bind runes**

Germanic runes **Anglo Saxon additions** **Bind runes**

APPENDIX II

The following impressions were the result of an experiment, an attempt to know the runes intuitively, without the censor of reason.

On 24 consecutive nights a circle was cast, and each rune successively invoked and meditated upon. A written communication was invited from the rune gods. What was given in answer is here recorded exactly as it was received.

There were sometimes temptations to alter the wording of lines for the sake of clarity. These were resisted. On occasion two words would occur simultaneously to describe a single thing. Both were recorded, and the one that later seemed most meaningful selected.

Exactly what the communications mean, and whether they possess any intrinsic value or beauty, is left to the judgment of each reader.

In the beginning was the great ox, Adumla
From her blood, the fruits of the earth
From her hide, the roof of the sky
From her bones, the mountains
From her milk, the sea
When she lowed, the sorrow of her voice
Shook the world like a vast, hollow bell
For she was naked, and alone
The fire ran to her, and danced in her womb
From its mouth issued a thundering river of voices
That shook the floor of ice and shattered it
Thus came the primal spring

Mine is the strength of mountains
My shoulders hold up the sky
My feet mark the four corners of the world
Hear me and tremble, puny ones
My hoofbeats are thunder
Where they strike the stones the lightning speaks
And caverns are riven deep between the hills
What man shall measure my majesty?
Or dare the fire of my flaming glance?
You flee before me!
I grind your bones, and sew the earth with your blood
My roar of triumph eats the shrill cries
That die in your throats
I sneer at your deceitful wiles
Caught in your pits, I bellow defiance
Unbowed, unbowing, the beat of my heart
Is the drum-dance of life-lust
Fools!
When you slay me, I win

Pain!
Rolling red circles of agony
My pain is in the stones that crack
With frost in the mountains
And bleeds from the stumps of wind-downed trees
Hunger is my name
Murder my right hand; hatred my left
My smile reveals the teeth of the serpent
Coiled in the soft belly of night
My voice is a whisper
My truth a lie
Let me share my pain with you
I will bathe you in molten fire
And scrape your nerves with the keen steel
Of my laughter
Lovers of the night, lie with me
In the velvet arms of my shadow embrace
My kiss will fill your throat with poison
My tongue, venomous as the serpent's
Black with death

The children come to me
They gather around with eager, upturned faces
What stories I have to tell them!
What mysteries to unfold
I was old when the land was young
When the hills rose up, my beard was black
When the sea came and covered them, my beard was grey
Now in these ancient days my beard is white
With snow on snow of many winters
While the world was yet young
I looked on everything and wondered
My eyes drank in the endless rolling oceans
And are blue as the cloudless sky
I heard the music of birds, the song of beasts
The deep whisper of trees and mantra of stones
And my words are simple and true
Come to me, foolish child
Let me embrace you
Let me dry your tears
We will laugh together about nothing
And be young in our hearts

The chill of autumn quickens your blood
And sets your feet to wandering
I am the long road that has no end
The distant vision that fades like morning dew
On I lead, ever onward
Until you are heart-weary of world-wandering
And sick of miles beneath your feet
Close your eyes
Let your beast guide you
Through the forest of shadowed desires
The thicket of fears
The wasteland of years wasted
You have no home before you or behind
The place you were has vanished into dreams
The place ahead mocks you as it recedes from hope
Your heartbeats are the hoofbeats on the stones
Of my cold heart
I spur you ever onward, restless rider
And the hunger in your soul
Is bitter wine of my blood
And coarse bread of my bones

Where I am, shadows are not
They flee before my face
Yet linger lurking at the edges of my power
Drawn to me by dark desire
They ken not
The silence in my voice
The space between my words
My children, black of face
I give them birth
Then kill them with my love
They flutter in their madness
Groaning to fly free
Agonized by their destiny
Struggle to escape
They come to me
Always they come to me
Who am heart of their desire
The secret flame, the spark of hope
The star that guides them home
And gives them peace

Give me freely of your heart
I will witness you
And stand by you when the tale is told of your life
Before the Ancient Ones
And speak for you when your tongue is mute
None can force me from you
But if you covet me, I am not
Unless another give me you
I am love, and pain, and joy, and tears
In all of these, yet not these things
Only when you cease desire
Will I come to you
When hope is forsaken and you bow your head
Will I embrace you as my love
And bittersweet love draw from you
Making ice to burn and melt to air
A joyous dancer on the winds
To sing to you and beckon
Laughing
To banish vain regret

Bathe me in soft light
Come to me in pleasing raiment
Wearing scents that sanctify
Your eye is filled with gentle love
Your song a lullaby
Make for me a wedding bed
My breast your pillow
My arms to cover you
Through the mysteries of agony and delight
You come to me
Eyes wide and wondering
Heart a dry chalice open and thirsting
For the shining silver dew of my breath
Wisdom unspoken, unpenned, undreamt by man
There are no shadows in this place of misting grey
No edges harsh to cut and pierce
No teeth, no nails, no crowning thorns
Shall mar your perfect form
Child of the upper reaches
Far marches of the soul
Descend to me
Ascend to me
The circle is complete

Heart of stone and fist a heavy hammer
Again and again I beat you down
As many times you rise, I strike
Hear the roar of my triumph!
It eats your puny cries for mercy
My tears cut you down in the furrow
Make black your shoulders and your crown
Ahrr-roar-ah-roar-ooh!
How mighty is the voice of winds
It thunders on the distant mountains
And rings like falling axes on the trees
It cracks the stones and slaps the face of waters
The weak tremble, the strong cower
Master of the sky
Ruler of the earth
None dare lift their eyes to me
I walk alone
And rule in grandeur of solitude
Bitter victory
To rule a barren, empty land
It is my right, my mighty curse
Never will I bow my head
Ahrr-roar-ah-roar-ooh!

When all is stripped away
And honor lies in the dust
Dignity burned to ashes, hope drowned
Vanity tattered in the wind
Trust a dim memory of a forgotten dream
When even pain deserts you
And senses merge and blur
Sounds a dull thunder of dark water
All colors grey, tastes all bitter
Your fingers mute, your cries lost
Eyes unseeing and unseen
When you stand stripped to the bone
With nothing
Utterly alone
Still I am with you
Call to me, I come to you
Sleep in my arms, I carry you
To bear you up when you sink
To force the air into your mouth
When you hunger after death
You cannot escape too freely
Your duty

Silent as madness, murderous patience
Wait for the slip
The careless word, the thoughtless act
Wait for the fall
It will come at last
When the heart is light and gay
When lovers dance
And dreams draw near enough to touch
Almost
Neither look before you step
Neither think of what you do
Or what is done to you
The end is not far, only look
How near it seems
Reach to touch, farther, only reach
It waits for you
The other side of the shadow
Bold as laughing children
You slide between my teeth

The sleek fox running on the fallen tree
The hawk that rises above the cliff
Darting dragonfly reflected in the pond
Dreaming willow gliding fingers in the brook
Smoke that rises between tall dark firs
The ring of axes, steel on wood
A distant song, the midday heat
The moving clouds, the rustling grass
The sun-warmed rock you sit upon
The ant crawling beside your hand
Scent of wildflowers, flash of butterfly
Look—there am I
Turn—I am gone
Drifting on the wind, swimming in the stream
Leaping on the flash and spark, still within the earth
Rise and fall, spin and step
Dance with me, I lead you on
I cannot stay, you must follow
Always follow, never touch
Follow, follow, faithful suitor
Always wooing, never winning
But if you stop and close your eyes
I was with you all the while

Ancient sentinel of the doorway
Between the shadows and the light
Stand I, strong in years
I watch, and am silent
Where I am, there is a way in
And a way out
A guide that will not fail
Deep roots draw power from hidden spheres
Magic lies locked in my heart
I bend, I do not break
The bolt flies to the center of desire
In the silence, old songs are sung
Mossy with ages, groaning with eons
To the mute dead in the resting cells
Their flesh my food
My thoughts, their memories
My nerves and sinews hem them down
In the dark womb of their mother
But carry whispers of change
Murmurs of hope
From the face of the sun

In the tree, a fruit
In the fruit, a tree
Give thanks to the golden child
For sweet white flesh and crisp red meat
As the seed of the tree is bound in sweetness
The seed of man lies wrapped in desire
To plant the seed, eat the fruit
Sometimes bitter, sometimes over-ripe
No way to know until you taste
Once plucked, kept for life
The seed cares nothing for the fruit
The fruit does not regard the tree
Yet all are one
And when you pick my shining stars
You are one with me

Away! Fly away! Flee!
Do not draw near, you cannot pass
This way is bounded
I am the end
My arms hold up the heavens
My feet are deep in the earth
I am the last and the first
Met in the circle
The gap in the ring
The stop after the final word.
I am the tree of secrets
That tells not
The Ancient One hung upon
And looked past my roots
Only he dared to gaze
Behind the fearful thought
To the bold man, hope
To the coward, shame
Touch me not!
For I am death of the soul

The word is light in darkness
Fire in long winter's night
Darting like the serpent
Lashing the mute stones
Shattering numb repose
I am the tongue of the Shining One
My voice is thunder
All ways open before me
There is no hiding place
No flight swift enough
I flash on the talon of the hawk
On the gleaming tooth of the wolf
In the eyes of the true man
Cover your face with your hands
Pretend you cannot see
I raise the stench of your vanity
But embrace me to your heart
And I make you pure and clean

What is stronger than truth?
No work of stone can survive it
No lying words dispose it
Truth endures to the end of things
All else is fleet and passes away
All that subsists is truth
Cruel dart that pierces every shield
Without pity, without remorse
Truth is, it cannot be other
What dares defy it is destroyed
Slayer of false dreams and false hope
Hard master, but equal in justice
All must serve, all are slaves
Truth is the highest King
Who holds all honor bound
Truth is Lord, holy truth
Disdain all lesser powers
In pain is wisdom, in loss is triumph
I the herald, speak His Word

Green runs the sap in trees
Green the leaves, green the tender buds
All sing the sun's return
And dance a circle to honor him
Bend and sway in the scented breeze
Dance with me by swollen brook
All death is fat with new life
I am midwife for bringing it forth
I ease the groaning and the sighs
Bring gentle smiles to pallid lips
Sweet breath to hollow lungs
Make strong the rhythm of the heart
Show the fish where to swim
The birds where to fly
The eye where to search
The blood where to flow
Quickener of all life am I
At my touch the seed falls
The flower blooms, the fruit swells
I am the oil that turns the wheel of earth
Upon the axle of the moon and sun

Swift foot runner
Through winding valleys, across barren ridges
Where the heart fears to go in boldness wandering
Strong is my back to bear you up
Doubt is my burden, fear my rider
High above the serpent's dart I bear you
Above the poison sting of venom thorn
My hoofbeats are thunder
Strike sparks from the frozen face of stone
Where the road ends I am the way
Go boldly out from vale of dreams
With steel test your vision golden
Win the jewel, bear her safe
My back can carry two
When you weary and you sleep
I will lead you home

In craft is one way, in cunning another
In courage a third, endurance is four
All ways lead through me, I am the door
Why do you wander? I am the center
Come home to me. Why do you roam?
Seek here the answer, no matter the question
Here is the reason whatever the purpose
Words that are wisdom, fingers that weave
Twist pain into pleasure, loss into gain
Heart sore with learning and gladness of knowing
All that is living I hold in my hand
Flowers and kingdoms, mountains and sand
Mine is the shaping, merriment making
I am the Yes in the silence of No
Do not deny me, I am your savior
I am your picture, I am your mirror
I am your laughter, I am your I

Soft to caress, hard to strike
Bent by the wind and warmed in the sun
Look at me straight, you will see my heart
Glance askew and get only lies
Gentle in love, men fear my rage
Cut me or break me, always I am
Visions flowing into your sleep
Stone and clay that dreams are made on
Listen to me, my bubble of voices
All that has been lies within
All impressions made on my skin
Fade, but are never forgotten
Patient I work, time is my measure
Always my circle, no end to begin
To take the easy way, to embrace resistance
Or to shatter it, if it will not relent
I am the strongest because I resist nothing

Shed no tears that I am departed
Across the sea in my golden car
In the fire that you build to cook your meat
In the thatch you raise against the rain
In the strong stones that wall your keep
In the stout door barred against the night
I abide, in the eyes of your children
From my heart the good corn grows
The waters in my well are sweet
The dog that lies across your step
Remembers me, and I him
When his bark rings joyfully
I am come to be with you again
The children of my flesh
Guard well my ways, despise them not!
No look so fair as the look of love
In the eyes of one returning

Shadows depart
The hidden is revealed
Forget your fear, born of ignorance
All will be made clear to you
There is no threat under the light
What seemed conflict is harmony
Fearful cries, the half-heard music of birds
Hulked shapes, the stones in the field
Malicious whispers, only the wind
I am ever with you and in you
The morning brings remembrance
The twilight of your long sleep
Round as a mother with child
Your eyes open—you see me
Your lids shut—you forget
I am unmoved
Turn like the millwheel on its spine of oak
I do not turn away from you

Mingle with your blood the earth of your father
Who has shed his fire in the bowels of your mother
The place subsists from son to son
Demarked by memory, fixed by valor
From this dust your flesh is nourished
By bones of your race the fields are green
In turn you will nourish the yew trees
Stand firm as the deep set rock
Your roots reach the mouths of heroes
Honor to die for their sacrifice
Or what they won will be stripped away
What is held by will is taken by will
The circle broken,the vow undone
At the end of being your only earth
The dust you carry, ashes of shame

On the following pages you will find listed, with their current prices, some of the books now available on related subjects. Your book dealer stocks most of these and will stock new titles in the Llewellyn series as they become available. We urge your patronage.

TO GET A FREE CATALOG

You are invited to write for our bi-monthly news magazine/catalog, *Llewellyn's New Worlds of Mind and Spirit*. A sample copy is free, and it will continue coming to you at no cost as long as you are an active mail customer. Or you may subscribe for just $10 in the United States and Canada ($20 overseas, first class mail). Many bookstores also have *New Worlds* available to their customers. Ask for it.

In *New Worlds* you will find news and features about new books, tapes and services; announcements of meetings and seminars; helpful articles; author interviews and much more. Write to:

Llewellyn's New Worlds of Mind and Spirit
P.O. Box 64383-L826, St. Paul, MN 55164-0383, U.S.A.

TO ORDER BOOKS AND TAPES

If your book store does not carry the titles described on the following pages, you may order them directly from Llewellyn by sending the full price in U.S. funds, plus postage and handling (see below).

Credit card orders: VISA, MasterCard, American Express are accepted. Call toll-free in the United States and Canada at 1-800-THE-MOON.

Special Group Discount: Because there is a great deal of interest in group discussion and study of the subject matter of this book, we offer a 20% quantity discount to group leaders or agents. Our Special Quantity Price for a minimum order of five copies of *Rune Magic* is $51.80 cash-with-order. Include postage and handling charges noted below.

Postage and Handling: Include $4 postage and handling for orders $15 and under; $5 for orders *over* $15. There are no postage and handling charges for orders over $100. Postage and handling rates are subject to change. We ship UPS whenever possible within the continental United States; delivery is guaranteed. Please provide your street address as UPS does not deliver to P.O. boxes. Orders shipped to Alaska, Hawaii, Canada, Mexico and Puerto Rico will be sent via first class mail. Allow 4-6 weeks for delivery. **International orders:** Airmail – add retail price of each book and $5 for each non-book item (audiotapes, etc.); Surface mail – add $1 per item.

Minnesota residents please add 7% sales tax.

Mail orders to:
Llewellyn Worldwide, PO Box 64383-L826, St. Paul, MN 55164-0383, USA

For customer service, call (612) 291-1970.

THE NEW MAGUS
The Modern Magician's Practical Guide
by Donald Tyson

The New Magus is a practical framework on which a student can base his or her personal system of magic. This book is filled with practical, usable magical techniques and rituals which anyone from any magical tradition can use. It includes instructions on how to design and perform rituals, create and use sigils, do invocations and evocations, do spiritual healings, learn rune magic, use god-forms, create telesmatic images, discover your personal guardian, create and use magical tools and much more. You will learn how YOU can be a New Magus!

The New Age is based on ancient concepts that have been put into terms, or metaphors, that are appropriate to life in our world today. That makes *The New Magus* the book on magic for today. If you have found that magic seems illogical, overcomplicated and not appropriate to your lifestyle, *The New Magus* is the book for you. It will change your ideas of magic forever!

0-87542-825-8, 368 pgs., 6 x 9, illus., softcover   **$12.95**

THE POWER OF THE RUNES
A Complete Kit for Divination & Magic
by Donald Tyson

This kit contains *Rune Magic*, Tyson's highly acclaimed guide to effective runework. In this book he clears away misconceptions surrounding this magical alphabet of the Northern Europeans, provides information on the Gods and Goddesses of the runes, and gives the meanings and uses of all 33 extant runes. The reader will be involved with practical runic rituals and will find advice on talisman, amulet and sigil use. This kit also includes the Rune Magic Deck. This set of 24 large cards illustrates each of the Futhark runes in a stunning 2-color format. This is the first deck ever published, which makes it not only unique, but truly historical!

A set of four, square, wooden rune dice, designed by Tyson, are included. The user casts them down, then interprets their meanings as they appear before him. With the 24 Futhark runes graphically etched on their sides, these dice let the user perform an accurate reading in mere seconds.

0-87542-828-2, Boxed set: *Rune Magic*,
24-card deck, 4 dice w/bag   **$34.95**

Prices subject to change without notice.

A PRACTICAL GUIDE TO THE RUNES
Their Uses in Divination and Magick
by Lisa Peschel

At last the world has a beginner's book on the Nordic runes that is written in straightforward and clear language. Each of the 25 runes is elucidated through no-nonsense descriptions and clean graphics. A rune's altered meaning in relation to other runes and its reversed position is also included. The construction of runes and accessories covers such factors as the type of wood to be used, the size of the runes, and the coloration, carving and charging of the runes. With this book the runes can be used in magick to effect desired results. Talismans carved with runescripts or bindrunes allow you to carry your magick in a tangible form, providing foci for your will. Four rune layouts complete with diagrams are presented with examples of specific questions to ask when consulting the runes. Rather than simple fortunetelling devices, the runes are oracular, empowered with the forces of Nature. They present information for you to make choices in your life.

0-87542-593-3, 192 pgs., illus., mass market   **$3.95**

RUNE MAGIC CARDS
by Donald Tyson

Llewellyn Publications presents, for the first time ever, Rune Magic Cards created by Donald Tyson. This unique divinatory deck consists of 24 strikingly designed cards, boldly portraying a Germanic "futhark" Rune on each card. Robin Wood has illuminated each Rune Card with graphic illustrations done in the ancient Norse tradition. Included on each card are the old English name, its meaning, the phonetic value of the Rune, and its number in Roman numerals. Included with this deck is a complete instruction booklet, giving the history and origins, ways of using the cards for divination, and magical workings, sample spreads and a wealth of information culled from years of study.

0-87542-827-4, 24 two-color cards, 48-pg. booklet   **$12.95**